THE *girl* ON THE *wall*

By Preeva Adler Tramiel

AYT PRESS
PALO ALTO, CALIFORNIA

AYT Press
555 Bryant Street, #477
Palo Alto, CA 94301
www.aytpress.com

The maps of Europe 1933, Hungary indicated, Hungarian Expansion, and Einsatzgruppen massacres in Eastern Europe are reprinted with permission of the United States Holocaust Memorial Museum.

The "Age of Asparagus" is reprinted with permission of Stan Lipsey and Nissen Chackowicz.

The lyrics for "Broadway Shabbat" are reprinted with permission of Mark Goldstein.

Quantity sales. Special discounts are available on quantity purchases by corporations, associa-tions, and others. For details, contact the "Special Sales Department" at the address above.

Orders by US trade bookstores and wholesalers. Please contact BCH: (800) 431-1579 or visit www.bookch.com for details.

Printed in the United States of America

Cataloging-in-Publication Data

Tramiel, Preeva Adler, 1958- author.
    The girl on the wall / Preeva Adler Tramiel. -- Black
and white edition. -- First edition.
    pages cm
    LCCN 2015918123
    ISBN 9780996734301 (pbk.)
    ISBN 9780996734318 (ebook)

1. Tramiel, Preeva Adler, 1958- 2. Children of
    Holocaust survivors--United States--Biography.
    3. Sisters--Poland--Oświęcim--Death. 4. Jews--Ukraine--
    Mukacheve--Biography. 5. Holocaust, Jewish (1939-1945)
    6. Autobiographies. I. Title.

    E184.37.T738A3 2015   973'.049240092
    QBI15-600218

First Edition
20 19 18 17 16   10 9 8 7 6 5 4 3 2 1

For my parents, Chaya and Hershi Adler

Contents

Acknowledgments

I owe much gratitude to my cousin Sam Kahan and his wife, Tirza, for being friends, mentors, and partners in this journey of self-discovery, and my aunt Nina Petya Adler, for giving me some great tips for my research.

Many thanks as well to my editor, Jami Bernard who pushed, pulled, cajoled, and otherwise schlepped me through the first complete draft.

Eti Magal; Eshel Spiro *z"l* ("of blessed memory"); Eli and Ditza Maskit; and Yehuda Beinin all hosted me in Israel and gave me the courage to continue my journey.

I am also grateful to the congregants and staff of Congregation Etz Chayim in Palo Alto, California, especially Jessica Bernhardt and Ron and Bonnie Shipper, who encouraged my writing, and to a host of readers and helpers, including Maggie Douglass, Helen Page, Anne Heit, Lisa Jungherr, and Elspeth Olson. They all helped move the project forward.

My husband, Leonard Tramiel, taught me the power of numbers, precision, and persistence, and he is the love of my life.

My surrogate sisters know who they are. Thank you, ladies!

And, finally, I thank my big family of cousins. On my father's side I have Howard, Sam, Sy, Zippy, Doreit, Ronit, Erela, Ditza, and the late David and Asher, *z"l*. On my mother's side I have Louise, Robert, Rifki, Sandy, Hillel, David, Rebecca and Ariel, and the late Richard and David, *z"l*.

INTRODUCTION

Who Was the Girl?

There is an old Hasidic tale about a rabbi who asked God for miracles by going to a special place in the woods and reciting some magic words. He got the miracles he needed. When he died, his successor went back to the special spot in the woods. He didn't know the magic words, so he invoked the name of the first rabbi and asked God for miracles, and they came to him, also. When the second rabbi died, his successor sat in a chair in his study and pleaded. "God, I don't know the place in the woods or the magic words to ask you for miracles," he said. "All I know is the story of how it happened, and that will have to be enough."

And it was enough, because God loves stories.

If there was one thing my father had, it was stories. He put me to bed at night with tales of Europe and war and about his many acts of daring and heroism. I loved to hear about him jumping motorcycles and racing cars and standing up to the Germans. The stories were so enthralling I never thought to ask about the number tattooed on his arm.

One of his favorite stories was from the time of the German occupation of his town, Munkach, now known as Mukacheve, in Transcarpathia, Ukraine. He and his brothers took two liters of grain alcohol and made schnapps out of it, and then got four liters of alcohol, flavored it, and traded it for eight, and so on and so forth, until they had enough schnapps to trade for a satchel of coffee.

My father, the oldest, took that satchel to a German officer to do business. "When I opened that bag," my father said, "the officer's eyes got wide. He bent down and he *schmeked* ['smelled'] the coffee—ahh—deep, like this," he said, inhaling. Coffee was hard to find in their remote town at that time, even for Germans. In exchange, the soldier opened a door. "He took me into a room where my head went up and I *schmeked*—ahhh—even deeper, a wonderful smell," my father said. "It was a roomful of tires!" My father's family ran a taxi business, and the war meant rubber was in short supply. "We could fix cars so they ran on propane, even wood, but tires were like gold."

Then he would ask me "Preevaleh, did I tell you about how you recognized me from the moment you were born?" He had, of course, many times. But I could never hear enough of how I had made a special face at him from my hospital bassinet, proving that I have always known who my father was.

Me, I didn't like telling stories so much. I was embarrassed whenever I had to perform. Daddy was the storyteller, not me. On Fridays in the summer, when the days were very long, my father and I walked to synagogue together, three short blocks and two long ones to Webster Avenue in the Bronx. There he showed me off to his friends—squat old men with pomaded hair and hairy necks who spoke with gravelly voices in languages I did not understand.

"Tell them what your name means," my father prodded me.

I straightened my green jumper, focused my eyes dead ahead, and recited what we had practiced together: "My name is Preeva," I said. "When God created man, he said to him, *Pru u'rvu ee melu et ha'aretz*, 'be fruitful and multiply and develop the earth.'" The men made phlegmy coughs into their handkerchiefs and poked each other, as if my name were funny.

I loved my father's tales—about becoming a Russian soldier on a whim, driving tanks, fooling Germans—and figured he'd have another good one to explain the girl on the wall. She had a big white bow in her blonde ringlets, and she lived in a gilded frame on the wall over my parents' bed. She wore a smocked dress and had huge blue eyes that looked out at infinity. When I was very little, I could climb up on the flat top of my parents' headboard and balance against the wall for a closer look. I tried to stare her down, but she didn't blink. I had to pick my time carefully—my father and I were only alone together at bedtime, in my room, and I wanted to be in his room, looking at the picture, when I asked him about it. And I wanted to alone with him, which did not happen that often. My mother was stiff around the picture, as if it angered her.

"Who's the girl on the wall?" I would ask my mother.

"Ask your father," she said.

This only made me more curious. So one Sunday when Mom was out of the house, I went into their bedroom and called my father. He came into the room and I pointed to the picture.

"Daddy, who is she?" I asked, anticipating a good story.

"Your sister," he said, turning away.

I stared at the picture and wondered what I had done wrong. Why had my father turned away? Why was he making a noise like sobbing?

Asking about the girl on the wall had been a mistake. Deep down, in a place I kept secret, I started to hate her.

One Sunday, my father was telling me a story of how he had created a shelter for a family of Jews in a garage he was maintaining for the Germans. "I took the wheels off a truck so it couldn't be moved, and they hid behind that truck until the war was over."

"Hershi," my mother scolded him. "Stop feeding her this nonsense."

"It's all true, every word," he protested.

"I don't believe you. If it's true, then what happened to these Jews you hid and saved? Where are they today?"

"In Brooklyn. They're in the phone book."

My mother hauled out the doorstop white pages—she kept a phone book for each of New York's five boroughs—and looked up the name he had given her. She made a phone call. Then we piled into the Chevy and drove to a leafy street lined with brownstone buildings. The family there welcomed my father into their home like the hero he claimed to be.

All I have of that day is the memory of a tree outside their window, a carved wooden chest of drawers, and a slice of birthday cake with frosting. That's all I have. I can't even remember the family's name. I had the proof right there that my father's stories were true, and I lost it through my own carelessness.

In the story about the magic words in the woods, the rabbi asks for miracles. The only miracle I ask is to have my father back, and I know it is not possible. But I still have a few of his stories, and that is going to have to be enough.

PART I

A Child of Survivors

CHAPTER 1

A Leaf under Ice

My father

My father was a tall, strapping man with dark brown hair, broad shoulders, a strong jaw, a face tanned dark from years of working outdoors, and eyes that my mother called the color of a leaf under ice. He had a number tattooed on his arm from the concentration camps and seemed to have already lived several lifetimes before he walked into a Bronx candy store at age forty-five and saw my mother working behind the counter. "I walked in to buy a pack of cigarettes, and I walked out with her heart," was the way he told it.

When my parents were first married, they lived in a walk-up on Hunts Point Avenue close to the corner lot where my father ran his own auto-wrecking yard, what today might be called a salvage yard. Daddy bought and towed broken and abandoned cars from the driveways and roadsides of New York and dismantled them for parts. He called himself a junkie, stockpiling some parts for repairs and selling the rest to Bronx Iron for scrap. He built up his business from a literal hole in the ground, at first by flagging down dump trucks with clean fill and diverting them to his lot to gradually fill the hole until the property was level. Then he planted a hand-painted plywood sign to mark the existence of Adler Auto Sales. In time, his company shipped used parts all over the world.

Even after we moved to Tower Gardens Building One, we were close enough to "the place" that when the roads were closed for snow my father could walk to work. He rose early, often before dawn, and came home after 6 p.m., only taking Sundays off. He paid neighborhood fellows a few dollars to keep an eye on the business when he wasn't there, but for guarding the inventory he maintained a pack of dogs from strays he picked up along the seashore (as he said, "That's where the meanest ones live"). He made his own dog food by mixing stale bread and canned mackerel with water or milk and served it on clean hubcaps, one for each dog, all of whom he called Mookie. At any given time up to a dozen Mookies lived on the lot.

It was a good business but hard work. My father's hands were big and hard, and his fingers had little black lines of grease caught deep in the scars of the cuts and cracks that came from working with car engines, metal, and sharp tools. My mother washed his clothes with lye to get the grease out, and he wore a funny kind of underwear that I later learned was an athletic supporter—very thick with stripes, to keep from getting a *killeh*, or "hernia."

He was very proud of his muscles. He would hand me an old paring knife while I sat on his lap at the kitchen table and flex his biceps: "Go ahead, Preevaleh, test it." I never knew whether his muscle was really so strong that a knife couldn't penetrate it or if I simply couldn't bring myself to push hard enough to hurt him.

My father spoke many languages, especially when he didn't want me to understand what he was saying. One day, my mother and I decided to count them.

I had been complaining about having to learn Yiddish in the fourth grade at Kinneret Day School. They were already teaching me Hebrew there. "Ma, another language, it's not fair!" I complained.

It was a late afternoon, the time when you turned on the lights in the kitchen but didn't need the lights over the table. "You can learn as many languages as you need to," my mother said. "Your father speaks so many."

It was another in a growing number of family mysteries, why my father could speak to almost anyone, anywhere. Another mystery was why some people called him Adler Hershi and others, Hershi Adler (he was even Herman or Hermann to some and Samuel Adler on legal documents). Each morning, my mother and I kissed him on his way to work and said a few lines of mixed Yiddish and Hebrew as a goodbye blessing: *Gay gezint, und kim gezint, adonay matzliach darkehcha* ("go out well, come back well, and may God send you luck on your path"). I loved to repeat the mash-up phrases my father taught me, nonsense like, *Igen, migen, hopp de fliegn* ("yes, I don't know" in Hungarian, plus "catch the flies" in Yiddish). I could also say, *Nem to do madjaru beselnyi* ("I don't speak Hungarian") in such a good accent that Hungarians didn't believe me and started chattering in that up-and-down way they had, while I stared blankly.

He taught me phrases in Russian: *Kak po zhe vay it cheh, tovarish?* ("How are you, Comrade?") and *ocheen kharasho, nichivo* ("pretty good, I don't know").

One day I overheard my father exclaiming, "*A zopahd pitchok meen da nedet!*" When my mother heard me repeat it, she stopped what she was doing.

"Preeva, where did you learn that?" she demanded.

"Daddy said it."

"Hershi-ee!" my mother called. "A little girl should not say that."

"Say what?" I asked. "*A zopahd pitchok meen da nedet*?" I later learned that it meant—well, never mind.

On Sundays, we listened to the Yiddish station WEVD, "the station that speaks your language." My parents spoke Yiddish to each other, but in different dialects. My mother used Litvak, from the region around Vilnius. My father spoke something closer to Galitz Yiddish, used by the Jews of Poland and Galicia. As in to-may-to versus to-mah-to, the difference is heard in the sound of the vowels.

"*Litvak!*" my father would exclaim, "*Du redst nish kine richtigier Yiddish*" ("You don't speak proper Yiddish").

"*Galitzianer,*" my mother would shoot back, "*Du redst nish kayn richtiger Yiddish.*"

At the kitchen table, when my mother finally consented to help me count up how many languages my father spoke, we started with English. "And Hebrew and Yiddish and Hungarian and Czech and Russian and German," I said, as she jotted it down.

"Also Spanish," she said. "He uses it with Garcia," the man who replaced windshields and rented business space from my father. "And your daddy knows some Romanian, Polish, and Ukrainian from when he lived in Munkach." My father's hometown had been like a language school, since it had changed hands so often between Austria-Hungary, Hungary, Czechoslovakia, and the Soviet Union. "Oh, and Romany, the language Gypsies use."

"Daddy knows Gypsies?" I asked. I only knew Gypsies as characters in black-and-white movies: men in embroidered vests, women who wore spangled headscarves and played tambourines.

"From the concentration camp," my mother said.

I hadn't known that Gypsies had been in the camp, too, but I knew plenty of Jews besides my dad who had been: my uncles Willy and Imi, and my aunts Blanka (a.k.a. Batya) and Petya. Every year in school we had assemblies and sang songs to remember the people who died in the camps.

"There's also Italian," my mother said. "That's thirteen. Satisfied? Now go study your Yiddish."

It was my fourth-grade teacher Mar Borovic (*mar* is "mister" in Hebrew) who taught me Yiddish. One day, he gave me a note to bring home, addressed to Mrs. Adler.

"Preeva, what did you do now?" my mother roared. For the most part, I was an inattentive student, and she was probably thinking of the time I stuck a chewed blue pen cap in my ear canal while I was pretending to be Lieutenant Uhura from *Star Trek*. "Do not move an inch while I read this," Mom growled. "You're lucky I'm not *my* mother. She would have hit first, opened the letter second."

She studied the message and then looked up at me. I was still waiting for the slap or the slipper, but Mom's voice turned soft, and she showed me the note. "Preeva has been an excellent student today," it read. "She has paid attention in class and been very helpful and respectful."

I think the note had something to do with the day we learned Kaddish. One day, Mar Borovic brought in his mandolin to accompany us as we sang.

Mar Borovic had blue eyes and a brown comb-over. He usually wore a blue suit and had a very soft voice that matched his character. He wrote Yiddish poetry and sang songs in Jewish cafés around the city. My mother said he was more suited to teaching college kids than us "wild animals," but one day he brought in a strange, beautiful instrument—a wooden teardrop inlaid with dark and light wood and mother-of-pearl around the sound hole and on the fret board. He played his mandolin and then put it down to sing the Kaddish for us. "This is the song we sing to honor our dead," he said in a quavery voice.

"*Yisgadal v'yisgdash, shmey robbo*" ("Magnified and consecrated be the great name"), he sang in his soft tenor, covering his eyes and rocking back and forth.

After that day, I began to pay more attention to my books and to embracing Yiddish and the history that came with it.

My father and I in 1964, at Theodor Herzl's grave

CHAPTER 2

The Bronx Is Burning

When a steam hammer was set up on the marshy land across from our building on Bruckner Boulevard and began banging away, driving piles into the ground, it was a death knell for my Bronx neighborhood. Those piles supported I-beams that became the steel skeletons of public high-rise housing for lower-income families, but they weren't the only change my mother recounted in an increasing litany of doom: Southern Boulevard had become Bruckner Boulevard and then the Bruckner Expressway. Vacant property turned into used car lots and then public health clinics. Catalogs arrived listing properties that the city was auctioning off to recoup back property taxes.

The final straw was the fire. I was home sick from school one winter day in 1968, when it was so cold that frost flowers coating our casement windows became sheets of ice. The metal windowsills, so good for holding potted plants and supporting menorahs at Hanukkah, were terrible at holding in heat and had been covered with old towels for insulation. I was in the kitchen, amusing myself by peeling the thin sheets of ice from the window, when I saw a light in one of the windows of the big prewar apartment buildings that towered over a parking lot.

"Look, someone has a light on in the middle of the day," I called to my mother.

"That's not a light; that's a fire," she said.

She turned up station WINS on the radio. Then she picked up the phone and made a few calls. Her sources told her what was going on before it came on the radio. That fire was a six-alarm blaze that took out half a block of houses, the first of a long string of fires that turned the South Bronx from a collection of neighborhoods into fields of rubble.

Prewar buildings going up in flames inspired the 1972 BBC documentary *Man Alive: The Bronx Is Burning*. The fires continued through the World Series in 1977 when the cameras panned to the blazes surrounding Yankee Stadium and the announcer declared, "Ladies and gentlemen, the Bronx is burning." By then, like most of the neighbors we knew from those days, my family was long gone. In 1969 we moved to Yonkers, a dozen miles from the city, where my father's brothers Mendy and Willy lived.

Before we moved there, my parents drove around the neighborhood during Hanukkah, checking to make sure there were menorahs in at least some of the windows. They looked at properties for two months before they settled on a rental in a development of "garden apartments," where we lived on the ground floor of a red-brick, two-story building near a lake.

Life in Yonkers was very different from the Bronx. First, there were the shoes. When I needed new ones in the old neighborhood, Mom took me to nice little stores like Indian Walk Shoes in Parkchester, where the salesmen sat on stools with built-in ramps and measured your feet. I was encouraged to walk and run in the shoes to try them out, as long as I stayed on the carpet, and I always left with a good fit and a lollipop. In Yonkers, we went to Shoe King Sam and chose shoes from bins. When trying them on, you could only take very small steps because the shoes were tied together with a plastic string.

I didn't know a single person besides my family in Yonkers. Instead of trying to make friends, I often went to play with my cousin Seymour, "Sy," the younger son of my uncle Mendy and aunt Eva. Seymour's idea of fun was to toss a football around, but I was always jamming my finger and couldn't get my hand around the laces. I was no better at shooting hoops. I threw the ball straight up, and it came straight down and smacked me in the head. As a result, we mostly played indoors, reading Seymour's comics. Sy carefully tended and catalogued the collection, putting each issue in a special sleeve. I liked Superman and Batman. I also liked Captain America, a hero who had been frozen in suspended animation since World War II and was defrosted so he could fight alongside the Avengers. Sy was saving up to buy the very first Captain America, published in 1941, whose cover depicted the superhero punching Hitler in the face. "My parents fought Hitler," Sy told me. "They were soldiers in the Czech Brigade."

"My father was a war hero, too," I boasted.

"Yeah? Doing what?"

I put aside the comic I had been flipping through, where Superman visits a Bizarro world that exists in a parallel dimension, and went to find my aunt in the kitchen.

"Aunt Eva, what exactly did my father do in the war?" I asked.

She smoothed back my hair and sighed. "When your uncle and I were in the army, your father was in Munkach with his family," she said. "He was driving a taxi until the Germans took them all away."

"What do you mean, his family?" I asked. "Like, his brothers and sisters?"

"*Ach*, a tragedy," she said. "Don't tell your parents I told you, but he had another family before he met your mother."

"*Before*?" I didn't understand the word, because in my universe, the non-Bizarro one, there was no "before." There was only the moment I was born, when Daddy was forty-seven and Mom was thirty-five. I was *de kleine*, "the little one," the lonely only. My parents had wanted more children; I used to think my mother cried at night in her bedroom because I was so awkward with other people, but it turned out she had been trying and failing to get pregnant. My father was the type of man who would never see a doctor about something so private, and they were too old to adopt and never had the nerve or resources to take in a foster child, so I remained an only child.

Except, that was, for the girl on the wall.

I had long since stopped asking about her because when I did, my father, with his military bearing and care-worn hands, would always start to cry, and I felt it was my fault. So I learned to live with my confusion over how there could be a sister when everyone knew I was an only child.

"Your father had a wife named Suri," said my aunt. "And two children, a boy and a girl. They all died in the camps."

None of this made sense. Or, perhaps it did, but I didn't want it to, so I tucked the information away in a corner of my mind.

But even the hidden thought preyed on me. I began to imagine a parallel dimension in which the war had never happened, and the girl on the wall would still be alive. But that would mean my parents would never have met, and I wouldn't have been born. My very existence depended on another child dying horribly. I was alive in the world and in my father's heart, but she had been there first. No wonder she had remained his favorite, her likeness enshrined on the wall while mine was in a cheap frame on the dresser. Her life had been sacrificed for mine.

I pushed away a chilling thought: I only existed because of Hitler. I knew I was supposed to hate the man who had slaughtered six million Jews, but did I actually owe him something? Did I owe Hitler my life?

Burying this in the back of my brain didn't help matters when I found I was having trouble adjusting to public school. It wasn't at all like Kinneret, where everyone knew me, everyone was like me, and we learned Yiddish and Hebrew. I started in the middle of fifth grade at PS 26, a large brick public school. There were twice as many kids in my class as at Kinneret and only one teacher per day, instead of two or even three. The upsides were that I had only one language to worry about, we had recess on real grass, and the school stood near a little patch of woods where I could visit the snowdrops that poked their heads up out of the melting snow and hide from the larger kids that bullied me.

I had never experienced a public school Christmas. Our teacher got us excited for the season by having us make candy houses. All the moms came in to help, and I got to work with cardboard and scissors. I wanted to make a house that was modern, like the development by Moshe Safdie at Expo '67.

My final creation looked like two Fred Flintstone houses stacked together, with a wide terrace skirting the smaller upper module, an idea I had gotten from the picture of Safdie's Habitat that appeared under *A* for *architecture* in the one volume we owned of the *World Book Encyclopedia*. I broke the hooks off candy canes and used the loops and straight pieces to define the borders and beds of an imaginary flower garden. For the finishing touch, I covered the house completely in royal blue icing my mother had whipped up with her hand mixer.

"*That's* your candy house?" Mrs. Listi asked. It didn't sound complimentary. "It's quite, um, unusual. I mean, there's not much candy on it."

I looked around and saw that everyone else's houses were brown like gingerbread, with peaked roofs, and adorned like Candyland houses, or the gingerbread cottage in "Hansel and Gretel." Not one of them looked like a *real* house. I had never played the board game Candyland. Gingerbread houses were not in the *World Book Encyclopedia*, volume A. Still, I thought my imagination would be rewarded.

It wasn't. In another art assignment, when I tried to impress Mrs. Listi with a self-portrait that was a triptych—to show my many sides (me reading, me on the phone, me on a skateboard, even though I didn't know how to ride one)—she sent me out of the classroom to go talk to a nice lady who worked in the school yet was not a teacher. The nice lady and I did puzzles together and chatted.

"Vicki, listen," I overheard my mother saying on the phone later to her best friend, a former Kinneret mom. "They said there could be *a very disturbed child here.*" I assumed she meant a child in Vicki's household, not ours.

My father came home unusually early, and we all went together to the Jewish Family and Children's Service to meet with Devra Giges, MSW. Her office had lots of toys to play with—a dollhouse and coloring books and hand puppets. We took turns waiting in the outer office, while one of us went inside to see Mrs. Giges. When it was my turn, I squirmed at her questions: Whom did I play with? What did I like to read? Why didn't I like getting shots? They seemed pointless. I mean, who likes getting shots? But after a few visits, I began to notice some changes at home. My parents were talking to each other more. Suddenly my mother was encouraging me to go outdoors after dinner and play with the neighborhood kids in the "court," the grassy area in front of our new building. She bought me a watch and told me what time to come home, instead of just hollering for me out the window whenever she got nervous.

There were other changes that year, and the next, and the next. My father started wearing a robe when he hung around the house on Sunday, instead of lounging in his *gatkes,* "underwear." We saw Mrs. Giges less often, but the situation at home improved throughout the seventh, eighth, and ninth grades. My parents began letting me take the bus and subway to the city with friends from Westchester so I could meet up with friends from summer camp. A group of us would gather in Manhattan and go to Israeli parades, or picket embassies to "Free Soviet Jewry" ("Win valuable prizes!" we would jokingly say to each other). Political action led to social engagement, and I began going with groups of Habonim kids to gatherings as far away as Bensonhurst, Brooklyn. When I was in the ninth grade, I took Allegheny Airlines to visit summer camp friends in Montreal and Rochester.

When I got back from the visit to Montreal, the girl on the wall was gone from her place over my parents' bed. In her place was a picture of me.

The turmoil of the move to Yonkers and the family therapy were buffered by the stability of summer camp, which had been a constant force in my life since I had first started going at the age of eight. Habonim Camp Naaleh was a socialist Zionist camp in Red Hook, New York, where we spent our time doing the usual things—playing volleyball, making lanyards, singing silly songs—but also talking about Israel, history, class, and wealth. I hated it at first.

I was up in a maple tree reading *The Hunchback of Notre Dame* one peaceful day, the leaves shading me from interaction with other human beings. Quasimodo was in his usual perch in the bell tower, howling with grief, and it was time for *sicha*, "discussion group," an annoying activity that took place every day at 2:15 p.m., despite my dogged lack of participation. I planned to read right through it until the afternoon snack.

Some of the older kids plopped down in a semicircle at the base of my tree. The counselor leaned against the trunk. "Who here knows what social class is?" he asked. I leaned out over my branch to see and hear more clearly.

"Uh, a place where you learn about social studies?" one of the campers suggested.

"Not quite," said the counselor. "Think about the song we sing, 'Arise, ye prisoners of starvation.' It ends with 'The international working class will be the human race.' Class is a big group of people who are alike. It has more to do with who has money and who doesn't than with school."

"Hey, I know!" I said, climbing down. "If you have a place to live and enough to eat, you're middle class or upper class. I was just reading about it," I said, pointing to my Modern Library edition. "The priests and noblemen are upper class, and the people in the middle who have stores and stuff are middle class."

"What class are *you*?" the counselor asked me.

"Upper middle class," I said with pride. "My father took us to Israel when I was six, and I got an English racer bicycle for being brave when I got my shots."

The counselor seemed to think this over. Then he nodded and pointed to a place for me to sit, and for the first time, I joined the group.

When I returned from camp, I had my own songs to sing. My family had a tradition of singing Hebrew songs before eating Shabbat dinner together, and the ones I learned that summer turned out to be similar to the ones my parents had learned in the summer camps of their youths.

We'd start out the same way, together:

Ani v'at, at v'ani ("me and you, you and me")
Chaverim b' ("are friends in")

And then we would sing out the names of three different youth movements. My mother would sing:

Kibbutz Artzi.

My father would sing:

Ha-Betari.

And I would sing out:

Habonim.

So, Shabbat for me came to mean friendly competition ending in sweet harmony. After our sing-off, we sang the traditional song welcoming the Sabbath angels into the house, made the blessings over the wine and the washing of hands and the *challah*, and ate the only meal of the week we had together. After we ate, we sang again, our voices mingling and vibrating in my heart.

My family in 1973

CHAPTER 3

The Driving Lesson

Every visiting day at summer camp, my parents were stars—real-life *chalutzim*, "pioneers," who had been part of Israeli history. My mother had lived on a border kibbutz called Sasa in the early days of the state, and my father had fought in the Israeli War of Independence. They enjoyed the attention of *madrichim*, "counselors," who sat with us on our picnic blanket, transfixed by my father's stories and lured by my mother's generous lunch basket—at least until 1973.

"Did you make the roast beef with new potatoes and chives?" I asked my mother when the two of them arrived that year, the summer before I turned fifteen.

"I'm sorry; I didn't get a chance to cook," she said. "I brought you a sandwich from Epstein's Deli instead."

It was the first time my mother didn't bring a basket. It was the first time my father didn't tell any stories. We sat on a bench beneath a sassafras tree, where my father leaned back, arms spread, legs crossed, eyes closed. "His stomach is acting up," my mother said.

I came home after that summer to a household full of dread. Something was very wrong with Daddy. His doctor had put him on a bland diet and my mother called it an ulcer, but I had seen the posters and public service announcements for the warning signs of cancer: change in bowel or bladder habits, a sore that doesn't heal, unusual bleeding or discharge, thickening or a lump, indigestion or difficulty swallowing, obvious change in a wart or mole, nagging cough or hoarseness, and the kicker—unexplained weight loss. I wasn't sure about the warts and moles, but I silently checked my father's other symptoms against the list. "Hershi's losing his muscles and complaining about his pot belly. I don't know what's going on," I heard my mother telling her friends. "His doctor is a *sheester*," "a shoemaker," not a good doctor at all.

I finally confronted her. "Ma, why don't we get Daddy a better doctor?" I asked.

"Your father is comfortable with the one he has."

Comfortable. Who knew comfortable could be so bad for one's health? "You mean the same doctor who said you had the flu until you found out it was pneumonia?" I argued.

"Pre, there's nothing we can do. It's the way things are." The same determination that helped my father survive the Holocaust now kept him from changing his mind about his doctor.

By mid-November, when my father couldn't hold down any food at all, the doctor finally checked him into a low-rent hospital in a downscale Yonkers shopping center. The narrow lobby was really just a hallway, with six straight-backed metal chairs opposite a sliding window of the kind you see in factories and pawnshops. It smelled of phlegm and disinfectant. The first time I visited, I found my father with a tube in his nose and a stomach pump dripping brown goo into a jar by his bed. I could write my name in the soot on the windowsill where I set down the paper cup of violets I had picked for him. The only good quality this place had was that it was accessible by public transportation, since my mother couldn't drive, and my learner's permit was still months away.

"Can't we find a doctor who has privileges at a better hospital?" I asked my mother when we got home.

"No," she said. "Just pray they don't find anything."

But they did find something. My mother called it a carcinoma of the stomach, carefully pronouncing the entire phrase as if the scientific language would shield us from what my father really had: cancer that badly needed cutting out.

My mother chose the same surgeon who had operated on my *zaide*, her father, fifteen years earlier for colon cancer. Dr. Ginzburg was a "big" doctor, very much in demand, who nevertheless immediately booked us an operating room at Beth Israel—for Thanksgiving Day, no less. When he finally came out in his green scrubs and a solemn face, he told us he had cut out a third of my father's stomach. "We found secondary tumors a foot away," he said.

"Will he get better?" my mother asked.

He raised his hands and lowered them again in a gesture of helplessness. And still no one had said the word *cancer*.

I looked down at the cover of the textbook I'd been studying—black and yellow, with a magenta diatom in the middle. I vowed right then that I would become the best biology student in school, for Daddy.

And I was. I poured my whole being into studying science. While still in tenth grade, I took classes and tests meant for twelfth graders and got perfect scores.

My mother worried that I was taking on too much at school. I signed up simultaneously for Advanced Placement courses in calculus and biology and began looking for a part-time job. "It's okay, Ma," I said. "Pressure makes a diamond."

What I learned in Advanced Placement biology told me my father had cancer. The warning signs confirmed it. That my mother was looking for an oncologist screamed *cancer*, but no one in those days ever said the word aloud. "We're taking things one day at a time" was the delicate way my mother put it.

What could I do? I began taking it out on my geometry teacher. I rolled my eyes at Mr. Abrams whenever he asked a question. I drew nasty pictures of him in my notebook and made fun of him behind his back. On one occasion, I may have growled at him. The other kids changed their seats so they wouldn't have to sit near me. "What can I tell you?" my mother said to the school guidance counselors when she was invited in for a little chat. "Preeva makes trouble when she gets bored. Give her a challenge, and she'll behave."

They found me an after-school advanced math class. Although I did well, I didn't love it. I memorized the proofs like a script. Proof, the cornerstone of geometry, seemed impossible in a world where my father—my strong, honest, hero father—was weakening before my eyes. However, I stopped growling at Mr. Abrams, and the extra schoolwork distracted me from what was happening at home: my father was seeing an oncologist in Queens, and I was back to seeing Mrs. Giges, the therapist.

With all my father's medical bills, I assumed that summer camp was out. But somehow, when registration opened for Camp Naaleh the year I was slated to become a counselor in training, I was suddenly, miraculously able to enroll. It might have helped that my mother's friends the Lehrs were on the board of the nonprofit that ran and funded the camp. Their daughter Naomi was to be my bunkmate.

"Are you good, Sven?" Naomi asked when we rode up together on the bus from Union Square. Taking our cue from a comedy skit we had seen on television, we thought a Swedish accent was incredibly cool.

"*Ja*, sure," I said.

"So, Sven, I've got gossip. We're getting a new cook this summer, Hanna, a concentration camp survivor. My mom said she's from Hungary."

"*Ja*, they make great apple strudel in Hungary."

We never got to taste the strudel. When the new cook found she was responsible for feeding 150 kids three meals a day with no professional staff, just a rambunctious volunteer crew of campers and counselors who didn't know a chopping knife from a bong, she lost it. "*Fleishig*! FLEISHIG!

Not kosher!" she yelled at a camper who was about to add a pitcher of meat-flavored gravy to a pot of hot cereal made with milk.

"What, something's uncool with gravy?" said the perplexed camper, who was probably desperately missing bacon and hoping to add some flavor to the gluey oatmeal.

Hanna was angry, mercurial, often pretending not to understand instructions given to her in any of the languages she spoke. She took revenge on the kids who ridiculed her accent by making grey goulash out of every kind of meat that landed in her walk-in cooler. The silverware developed a thin coating of grease, and the infirmary was full. By the second week, the peanut butter and jelly reserves for the entire summer were gone.

Heshi, the *rosh*, "the head of the camp," sent for me during arts and crafts. "I have a surprise for you," he said.

"A package?" I asked hopefully.

"No, Preeva. Your parents will be staying here for a few weeks to help with the kitchen."

"But my dad fixes cars, and my mom isn't a cook."

"Your mother has experience in a kibbutz, so she knows how to organize things," he explained. "Your father speaks a million languages. Maybe the cook will understand one of them."

It was a little strange to have my parents staying a few bungalows over, but I was happily immersed in a theater group full of incipient comedians, having progressed beyond the previous summer when I managed to crack the dental retainer in my hip pocket during a vigorous improv session. We put on shows cobbled together from our chief influences: *Rowan & Martin's Laugh-In*, the Marx Brothers, and the nearby Borscht Belt. That summer we invented the character of Prince Plubzo, an improbable superhero who loved to eat. Plubzo had a ballad, sung to the tune of "The Age of Aquarius":

> When the meeeeeal is in the seventh course
> And hamburgers lie with peas

Then pieces of this vegetable
Are all that you can eat.
This is the dining of the Age of Asparagus,
The Age of Asparagus,
ASPARAGUS!

With my mother working in the kitchen, the utensils got cleaner, and everyone stopped getting sick. My father had less success. Even with his many languages, he could not get the cook to do anything differently. When Hanna suddenly stopped understanding her native Hungarian, my father switched to Czech, and when she forgot that, he switched to Russian, then to Romanian, but still we got goulash.

Naomi came running to report that my father had been in a terrible screaming match with the cook. "That isn't possible," I said. "Daddy never yells."

"You bet he yelled," my mother confirmed when I went to the kitchen to find her. "I've never seen him so angry. That ignorant woman called him a *kapo*."

"Ma, what's a *kapo*?"

"A Jewish prisoner who worked for the Nazis in the concentration camp—traitors, the worst kind."

By the next day Hanna was gone, replaced by a Chinese man named Richard who could make fried chicken so crisp and flavorful that all 150 of us stood up and applauded.

My parents stayed another week after the departure of the goulash queen. I was out on a walk in my Adidas and shorts, looking for fungus fans and Indian pipes—ghostly pale growths that glowed in the dark—when I saw the two of them on the hill behind the infirmary. They were strolling beneath the boughs of the birches, maples, and wintergreens, leaning on each other and swaying together with each step. I swayed back and forth a little too as I watched them go up the hill until they disappeared around a bend in the trail.

My father and I in 1975

That fall, my father began a course of chemotherapy. He developed sores on his arms at the injection sites and was fitted with an infusion pump to deliver the medicine straight to his liver. He wore it with resigned good humor and called it the *mashinke*, "little machine." Every day he filled it with medicine and wound it like a watch, using a little key. My mother gamely tended his wounds with tincture of benzoin and cleared a space on her perpetually crowded kitchen table so he could stretch out his arms and dry his sores in a patch of afternoon sunlight that came through the window.

He was sitting at the kitchen table with his arms outstretched when he called me to his side. "Preevaleh, now that you're old enough I'm going to show you how a clutch works," he announced.

"Finally, you're going to teach me to drive," I said, giddy with delight, but instead of taking me outside to the car, he drew something on the back of an envelope. It was a diagram of a "three on the tree" gear pattern, the type of clutch on our manual-transmission '64 Chevy. "Listen and learn," he said. The mechanic and former taxi driver in him wouldn't let me go until I could draw the diagram and name all the gears, all while the *mash-inke* was ticking away.

The tincture of benzoin smelled sweet, like cloves.

The following Sunday, early enough that I wouldn't endanger too many pedestrians, my father drove us to the parking lot behind Alexander's department store and let me take the wheel. "Remember, when you drive a car, you have power. Be careful how you use it," he said.

"Dad-deee, let me do it already!"

I shifted into second gear too quickly and lurched from one light pole to another. It took a lot of practice in the parking lot until I could shift through the gears with enough confidence to earn my father's highest praise: "You are Adler Hershi's *tochter*," my father's daughter.

Adler Hershi's *tochter* was ready for her time out on the city streets. It was an early fall day. The sky was overcast but bright, and the leaves were just starting to turn. I was planning to back out of our driveway and head for the junior high school half a mile away.

"Preeva," my father said as I unlocked the driver's side door. "If you want to drive, you have to learn to drive backward first. Reversing without hitting anything is harder, and more important."

"Huh?"

"Just use your mirrors."

"But, *backward*? The whole way?"

"It's your first time, so I'll let you turn your head to look. When you learn better, you'll just use your mirrors."

I put my arm behind the seat, turned my head, released the parking brake, let the clutch out, and drove slowly in reverse past the cars parked in front of Crestwood Lake Apartments, then up a small hill, around the cul-de-sac, and downhill—still going backward—putting my foot on the brake on the downhill to help me stay in my lane. I drove carefully past the intersection of Shoreview and Nassau and over the creek that emptied into

Crestwood Lake and was drenched in perspiration by the time we pulled in at Walt Whitman Junior High School.

"Good," said my father. "*Now* you can drive forward."

Maybe the driving backward, then forward, triggered my father's memory, because after about two blocks, just at the bridge where we stood every Rosh Hashanah to do Tashlich, "the ritual casting away of sins," he asked me to pull over. He put his face in his hands, while I wondered what was going on.

"*Oy*, Preevaleh," he said, without any preamble or explanation. "What we did in the camps for a lump of sugar."

He couldn't turn away as he had done when I was a little girl asking about the mysterious girl in the portrait over his bed. At the same time, I couldn't ask him what he was talking about because any mention of the camps brought up a flood of anger and despair. I had picked up this code of silence somehow from my father, aunts, and uncles and from years of indoctrination, disappointment, and guilt. We both just sat there till Daddy blew his nose and told me to drive home, which we did without incident.

* * *

My father died seven months later, ten days before the Regents Exams—what we used for finals—in my junior year of high school. This gave me just enough time to help my mother bury my father, get up from mourning, and take the finals for the toughest academic year I had ever had. As per the Jewish custom of sitting *shiva*, we covered our mirrors and received visitors. My mother and I sat on low cardboard boxes, but I was allowed to take friends into my room, and that is where I found myself toward the end of the mourning period with Robbie Gluckson, the most popular girl in my class. I was surprised she even knew my name.

"Let's make a list of who visited you," she suggested. "Here, I'll write it down."

I had no idea what she was talking about. I was a little dim about the concept of social capital and networking. My time had been spent reading and writing and doing math. So I told Robbie the first visitors that came to mind—the cohort of family members who were in my generation.

"Well, my cousins," I said, "There are eighteen of them."

"No, I mean from school."

I thought back and began ticking off names, these ones from chemistry class, those ones from the school paper, one or two from my part-time job as a cashier at a supermarket, a few from AP biology and history.

"Wow, even Alan," said Robbie, scribbling away. Alan Epstein was tall and strong and had a Mustang II.

Soon the list was two pages long. "Forty-five people, that's huge," said Robbie, the arbiter of such things.

I hadn't been that popular in the seventh grade, when my classmates tied me to a tree with my scarf. Perhaps pressure really did make a diamond. I was ashamed to think it had taken my father's death to finally make me sparkle.

CHAPTER 4

Be Fruitful and Run Away

1978, on Kibbutz Gezer

At Barnard College, which I chose because it was close to my mother, I thought I'd keep on shining. The Columbia Library had four million volumes. Everybody was a reader. For once my name did not stand out from the many Brookes, Chendys, Maryams, and Rumus at the college. I was just another girl with a strange name. It was a big relief to feel normal—until I started on the kosher meal plan and encountered rabbis-in-training who knew exactly what the name Preeva meant.

The kosher students ate dinner four blocks north of our dorms, at the Jewish Theological Seminary, where the American Conservative Jewish movement trained its (exclusively male at the time) rabbis. The cafeteria was full of them—all wearing *kippot*, "skullcaps," and pale from studying indoors. My first day there, one of them asked my name, and when I told him, I got the old look of shock I had been getting all my life. "Preeva means 'be fruitful and multiply,'" he said with a smirk. "I could help you with that."

Being Jewish at Barnard wasn't like being Jewish in Yonkers. In Yonkers it had meant you went to Hebrew school and your mother shopped at Syon Kosher Meat market. Not so at Barnard. Many of my fellow kosher diners, who also were my floor mates, had been educated in Orthodox *yeshivot*. They spoke in a strange sort of code, referring to Friday night as "*mitzvah* night," when married people were supposed to have sex. They wore knee socks, clogs, and denim skirts all the time. They traveled downtown to the Lincoln Square Synagogue on Wednesday evenings to hear Rabbi Shlomo Riskin give a *Sheer*, ("a teaching on a Jewish subject"). On Saturdays, forbidden by Jewish law from riding the subway, they walked the two miles to his synagogue to meet "yahmmies," nice Jewish boys in skullcaps, at services.

I stopped wearing my plaid wool shirt jacket with the patch that said *kosher* in Hebrew and abandoned the kosher meal plan—all to stay away from the yahmmies and the skirted girls hunting them for husbands. This strange new kind of Judaism had nothing in common with my reasons for keeping kosher or with the Zionist history I was proud of—or with me, for that matter. These girls were way more religious than I was and more studious. After dinner each night, they were either at the library or in one another's rooms giggling over a new color of highlighting pen.

My roommate, Gayle, was one of them. We had certain superficial qualities in common—she too was an only child, and we were both English majors, although my practical plan was to study economics, while hers was to be a social worker. Gayle was very sweet, but she drove me crazy. She subvocalized and moved her lips while she was reading, highlighting every other line with religious fervor. I tried to ignore it, but the low babble from the other side of the room sounded like pppppop mmmmhmahm sqreek sqreek sqreek pop pop hm hm sqreek.

"Could I turn on the classical station while we study?" I asked, hoping to mask the sounds. She said no.

"I don't go to the library because I need quiet to work," she said.

We tried to be friendly, but it was impossible. She was focused on proving that the religious teachings of the Zionist Rav Kook were the most lasting way to peace and freedom in the Middle East. I was focused on exploring the parties and freedoms of living on the Upper West Side of Manhattan. This included dating non-Jewish boys. When I introduced my mother to one, a fireman's son from Missoula, Montana, she said, "What a nice young man. You're not dating him, are you?" she asked me. "No, Mom," I lied.

Days after I moved into the dorm, my mother gave up our old three-bedroom garden apartment in Yonkers for a two-bedroom in Co-op City, in the Bronx, to save money and be near her old friends. She delighted in her view of Manhattan, her parquet floors, and the air conditioning included in the rent. But when my Yonkers friends came over, I saw the place through their eyes, and I wanted to cry—the yellowing vinyl slip-covers on the furniture and the unpacked liquor boxes serving as end tables shamed me. I began to spend as much time at college as possible, although I wasn't close to my floor mates, and I was starting to put on the "freshman fifteen"—extra pounds from the cafeteria's unlimited portions and the late-night runs for Häagen-Dazs.

My mother, sensing my unhappiness, took me upstate to Grossinger's for a long weekend. On a nature walk, I met a man who actually knew my father from his hometown of Munkach. "He was a taxi driver, right?" said the man. "I owned the Bata Shoe Store on the main street. I knew the other

Adler brothers, too—Mendy, Willy, Ludwig, and Imi. On Yom Kippur, they were the ones who chased the *goyim* away from the *shul* with tire irons."

I was secretly thrilled. My father, a tough guy, heroically protecting his community!

After that, I began to take a few risks of my own. I signed up for a ski week in New Hampshire, even though I had never skied before. After the first lesson, the older students who were on the trip persuaded me to try the intermediate slope, and I did. After that, they began calling me the Red Streak for the speed at which my cranberry-colored down jacket rushed by them. If my father could be a daredevil, so could I. I was Adler Hershi's *tochter*, and adventure was my birthright.

Now that I wasn't afraid to take chances, college improved. I took up theater and joined the debate club, the newspaper, and the cross-country running team.

And then I fell for Quentin Hebert.

Quentin was a tall, smooth-chested political science major from Texas. Oh, and he was Catholic.

The first time I saw him in a suit, I swooned. Everything else faded away in the glow of his flawless complexion (very pale) and his lips (very red). Quentin was my secret for nearly a year, but one summer evening when I was home for vacation, my mother opened the phone bill.

"Who is in Euless, Texas?" she asked.

"Oh," I said, "that would be Quentin."

"Like San Quentin? That is not a Jewish name."

"But, Mom, he's a really wonderful guy."

"*Y'mach shmo.*" ("His name should be blotted out.")

My mother never said, "If your father were alive, you wouldn't be dating a *shaygetz* ['non-Jewish boy']," but she might have been thinking it.

Defying my mother was one dangerous thing I did in my life—within limits. To please her, I declared myself an economics major instead of English, where my passion was. But I did not give up my *shaygetz*.

One night when Quentin and I were double-dating with my friend Tami and her hunky physicist boyfriend, we stopped on the street to say hello to a short, chubby guy with a paunch and a full beard. "Guys, this is Len. He works with me in the lab," Tami's boyfriend said.

After that, I ran into Leonard all the time. We ate in the same dives, went to the same movies. One time we both ran in the same ten kilometer charity race in Central Park. By then, I had realized that Quentin had no intention of getting really serious. Religion was just one of the obstacles. Oh great, I thought to myself, to a Catholic boy, I'm a *shiksa*. I saw my future with Quentin was limited, and we broke up. I never saw him again.

* * *

I didn't walk to my Barnard commencement. Late as usual, I ran— slate blue gown flapping behind me, hand on my head to keep my mortarboard in place. I barely made it to the ceremony; worse still, I was two papers short of a diploma. One was a paper on Victorian literature, the other a thesis in economics, and I didn't even have firm topics, let alone the forty pages apiece required for official graduation.

In many ways, I was feeling incomplete. I had no idea what I would do with my life, and my vision of the future after graduation was opaque. My earlier drive to do well in school and get out of the house and into a good college had been fueled by the impending loss of my father, and now that he was gone, I had no focus.

I took the LSAT just in case I decided to go to law school, but my score of seven hundred, though good, did not make up for my so-so college grades, so I never even filled out an application. I had always harbored a secret desire to be a writer and dashed off a last-minute application to the Columbia School of Journalism when I should have been en route to a debate tournament. Despite my lateness for the debate, I did well, but then I blew off a subsequent meet so I could try performing. Maybe I could do something in theater? I spoke with some off-Broadway producers for possible thesis topics, but the dismal economics of putting on a show, or even pursuing a career in acting, didn't appeal to me.

My first summer after college, I found a temporary job at a Jewish publishing house, where I spent half an hour each day on the phone with my mother, took every second of break time they offered, botched simple filing jobs, and was unsurprisingly not invited back after my three-month stint. I was living in an ancient fourth-floor walk-up that my mother called the Black Hole of Calcutta because the windows overlooked an airshaft. It was all I could afford, and I didn't want to take any of the money she offered.

I scoured the want ads and went on interviews and polished my résumé. I read *What Color Is Your Parachute?* and tried to focus on the hopeful parts.

* * *

A year later, life was looking better: I had a job at the *Wall Street Transcript*, a financial trade paper. I had moved in with a bunch of convivial roommates who had fixed up their apartment nicely enough so my mother approved of the premises. I had also somehow—or maybe he had done it—converted my casual friendship with Leonard into a relationship, to the point of meeting his parents for dinner and a show. For that date Leonard wore a suit, and I wore my best dress—a vintage, black velvet dancing number I had found at the Columbia University thrift shop.

I kept replaying in my head what Leonard had told me about them. They were named Jack and Helen. They had both been through the German camps. They were Polish, from a city called Lódź. Both were multilingual and had a colorful way with the English language. To match my own father's exclamation "Who the hell you are that you think you are?" which made Leonard chuckle, there was his father's expression, "Don't make a mountain out of a mohair," which amused me. They may have spoken like immigrants at home, but they did not look anything like my family. When we met them in the lobby of the Helmsley Palace hotel where they were staying, Len's mother was wearing a chic black dress and elegant shoes. His father was in full business attire, a silk handkerchief in his pocket and a cigar in his mouth, the very picture of a CEO. His parents walked so fast I had to struggle to keep up. I jabbered all evening out of nervousness, showing off my cookbook French. They seemed to like me anyway.

PART II

*Memories, Mysteries,
and Original Documents*

CHAPTER 5

Materialism and Its Contents

When I was six years old, I asked my father whether we were rich. We were riding up the elevator of our building in the Bronx after completing our weekly ritual of washing "the Sunday car," our new 1964 Chevy Impala, and my father was in his work clothes, a heavy cotton shirt and pants.

"Yes, Preevaleh," he said. "If you have ten cents more than you need, then you are rich."

My father and mother lived as cheaply as they could and never took on a cent of debt. They paid cash for what they needed and never wanted any more than what we had (or never let on that they did, anyway). My mother shamed me out of asking for the toys I saw on television commercials by parroting the advertisements back to me with dramatic emphasis, generous editorializing, and righteous anger. When I wheedled, "Mommy, it's only $19.99," she shot back, "*Only* $19.99 is more than its worth, and more than anyone should spend on a toy that lasts *two weeks*. Why don't they just add the extra penny and call it what it is, which is *twenty dollars*, those *goniffs* ['thieves']."

In the grocery store, my mother figured the cost per ounce of whatever we were buying, but she was also quick to explain to me how a boned piece of meat might be the better buy. She understood very well the concept of added value and the extra charge for processing foods and could analyze the worth of an item based on how easily she could make it at home. "If you want soda, we buy it," she said, "but iced tea we can make at home."

This consumer-oriented, humble attitude about money and life charmed my prospective in-laws. It was not the way they lived, though. The wedding guest list was finalized by my mother, my mother-in-law, and me, sitting in the kitchen of a corporate townhouse in Valley Forge, Pennsylvania. The reason we were in the kitchen, in a townhouse full of fancy modern French furniture, was that my mother could not fit in the chairs that surrounded the green-and-black marble dining table. The contrast in lifestyles and attitudes concerned me deeply. I had almost broken off the engagement because my parents and I had values we had picked up from our respective youth movements. We all believed in communal responsibility, strong Zionism, and the dignity of the working man. I had spent eight years in Habonim, going to summer camps and organizing a Westchester chapter. I had even gotten a letter of recommendation from the head of the movement that helped me get into Ivy League schools. I spent the summer between my sophomore and junior year of college in Israel, one month of which was spent volunteering on Kibbutz Gezer. (Heshi Gorewitz and Ken Bob, from my camps, along with other "Habos," members of Habonim, from all over the world, had started Gezer.)

In a real sense, the wedding was the final turning away from Habonim and Zionism. I wore the dress of my dreams: ivory *peau de soie* with a fitted bodice, full skirt, three-quarter sleeves, from Henri Bendel, on Fifth Avenue, instead of a discount house of some sort. And the ceremony and party took place at the Park Avenue synagogue.

To my shock, Habonim came to the wedding. My mother-in-law's uncle, Joseph Salsberg, turned out to be a founder of Habonim. "Uncle Joe" had been a member of Parliament for the Socialist Party in Canada. A respected friend of the family, he was conscripted into making the wedding toast. Joe took the microphone with great dignity, beaming with pride that his youth movement was finding its way back into the family. "I wish Leonard and Preeva only the best, and mazel tov," he said, looking out from under his bushy white eyebrows. He took a breath to say more, but I had already bounced up from my seat and thrown my hands in the air, shouting, "Yay!" Everyone applauded, and that was the end of Joe Salsberg's toast. I did not realize at the time that I had cut short a former member of the Canadian Parliament, but with a politician's feel for the crowd, he did not insist on resuming his speech after the cheering stopped.

* * *

Is there anything more materialistic than a wedding registry? At the insistence of relatives, Leonard and I filled one out. We got two full sets of pots, one from a person who worked for Leonard's father's company and one from a first cousin. Another first cousin, from Larchmont, bought me a set of queen-sized designer sheets that weren't marked with that brand I knew well from my childhood: "irregular." My mother, always careful with money, insisted on buying me the biggest present of all: a real silver flatware service for twelve, something she herself had never had. She yelled at me when I chose a simple, inexpensive pattern called William and Mary, by Lunt. "It's the cheapest set they make," she complained. "It's so plain."

"It's not plain; it's elegant," I said. I wondered what had happened to my mom, the ultimate value shopper, the anticonsumer, who had moved into Co-op City to save money, recycled *yahrtzeit* candleholders into drinking glasses, and never brought out the good dishes, so we ate off chipped glass ones from Woolworths. What happened to the woman who mended bed sheets by hand?

Marrying into Leonard's family was going to be a big change and not only for me. I had to figure out what to do with the bounty of household items that poured into my life. It was a far cry from my father's "ten cents more than you need and you're rich" minimalist approach to wealth. We got everything on our registry, plus three Cuisinarts.

CHAPTER 6

My Two Moms

Moving to Northern California gave me severe transplant shock—going from New York City to suburban life was hard. I was out of the habit of driving, and once I was on the highway, all towns tended to look alike. My husband was at work all day, and I was on my own to set up a house, which I had never done. I got the job of family coordinator, which my life as half of a duet with my mother had ill prepared me for. I have never known what to say to whom about plans, and plan making was doubly difficult, given my husband's dual role as a partner in the family business and his parents' son. For instance, on my husband's thirtieth birthday, his favorite cake arrived without its baker. My mother-in-law, Helen—petite, gracious, coiffed, well dressed, and a bit intimidating—had done a drive-by. She rang the bell that Sunday morning, put a marble cake in my hands, turned on her Gucci heels, and drove away in her red Jaguar.

"Len!" I yelled up the stairs. "Your mother just came with your cake and drove away."

"Why did she do that?" Len yelled back.

"She said she didn't feel good."

"Well, so?"

My husband's PhD in physics had not included work in human relations. "So, that's a totally made-up excuse. Something must be wrong," I told him.

The next day, I heard back from Leonard's older brother that Helen was mad at me. "Preeva didn't invite me to the party because I don't have a PhD," she had complained. I was confused. Hadn't Leonard invited his own mother to the party? Is the reason she brought a cake and then left in a snit because she didn't feel welcome in my house? I knew she was welcome; did I have to make it explicit?

Apparently, I did have to. When I had mentioned that some of Len's PhD friends were coming and had not invited her, Helen felt excluded. Someone had to smooth things over, and I knew it wasn't going to be Leonard. I drove down to Saratoga to be yelled at and to apologize for my thoughtlessness.

* * *

The marble cake incident in 1984 actually brought us closer, although there were many conflicts yet to come—like the Great Ski House Fight of 1985, when she accused me of leaving AIDS on the towels after our friends from San Francisco visited. Or the How Dare You Not Tell Me First fight of 1986, when my own mother was taken to a hospital on a Friday night for cardiac arrhythmia, and in the anxious night I spent making arrangements and worrying, I didn't get around to calling my mother-in-law until the next morning. Plus, there were all those minor skirmishes where I would mention an idea I had, and we would end up doing whatever Helen wanted anyway. They didn't call her the woman with a whim of iron for nothing.

Having a mother-in-law wasn't the same as having a mother nearby, my mother, especially once I became pregnant—which earned the highest possible praise from Jack: "Now you're in the manufacturing business!"

As a full-time mother I was home all day and up all night and so tired it hurt to breathe. Motherhood was the first job I had where I was responsible for something twenty-four hours a day, which scared me. In the dark hours of the night, I would hold my baby and realize I would die to protect him, which scared me even more. And then the dark thoughts

Only this face could get my mother out of New York.

came—demons out of my past, storm troopers and SS men somehow brought forward into today, and I wondered how I could hire workmen to create a secret hiding place under the house, just in case the Nazis, or something like them, rose again.

Of course I kept these thoughts to myself. My father-in-law, who loved a debate, would try to draw me into an argument, as he had for years:

"Hey, Preeva," he would say, "The Democrats are going to ruin the country."

"Whatever," I said, too tired to argue.

"You're not going to fight with me?" he asked, astonished. "What's happened to you?"

I wanted my mother.

When Len and I had flown east for a last look at a real autumn before impending parenthood grounded us, I had tried to convince my mom to move to California.

"Mom," I said. "I could really use your help when the baby comes."

"I'll think about it," she would say and then go on to talk about her sisters who lived a forty-five-minute drive away, and her friend Vicki who lived in the next building. I couldn't wait to get my mother out of Co-op City. It was no longer the working class utopia people had envisioned when it was first built on sinking land, with the busy New England Thruway just two hundred yards away and twenty stories down from her apartment on Darrow Place. The novelty of air conditioning and wood floors had long worn off, at least for me. The aluminum window frames in my mother's apartment leaked air and rattled in their coat of black soot and oxidation. The same winds that propelled the pleasure craft of the rich on Long Island Sound, at the yacht clubs two miles south on City Island and five miles north in New Rochelle and Larchmont, howled through the canyons of thirty-story buildings like ghosts on motorcycles. I had nightmarish visions of Mom getting blown over and rolling down the sidewalk, a large bowling pin in a blue raincoat.

During what I thought of as my last autumn visit, Len was parking the car while I was at a pay phone across from my mother's building. If I didn't call my mother before I rang, she might not hear the buzzer when I got to the door. An intimidating-looking young man who must have been over six feet tall came up to me. "Yo, you got a case quarter?" he said, holding out his palm a little too close to my seven-month-pregnant belly.

"A *case* quarter? What's that?" I asked.

I wondered whether Co-op City, a collection of ninety buildings on five hundred acres, housing more than twenty thousand people on the edge of Long Island Sound, had developed its own currency system while I had been off in California.

"You know, like, a quarter to make a phone call."

"Oh, you mean twenty-five cents!" I said. "Sure, but I need to call my mother first." While talking, I reached into my purse and handed the man his quarter. He took it and walked away, shaking his head, which was pretty much the response I got from my husband any time I opened my mouth. Still, even a minor shakedown like this on my mother's corner was all the more reason she should leave the Bronx.

Unfortunately, she and Leonard did not get along. When she visited us, for example, her relationship with our Amana Radarange got him angry. My mother had never seen a microwave oven before she saw ours, which was a fancy model with a carousel. She would put some food in it and turn it on just to watch through the glass as the dish revolved.

"Don't do that!" Leonard yelled. "Don't press your face up against it."

"Why not? I thought this thing was safe," my mother would say.

Leonard had worked with radioactive isotopes in graduate school. "It's safe if you stay about six inches away," he said. "Any radiation that leaks drops off really quickly by then."

"Does this thing make *radiation*?"

When Leonard tried to explain how the radiation cooked the food, he made things worse. "The Klystron tube is directed and there's shielding," he told her.

"So you're saying it's safe."

"Yes, but you shouldn't put your face up so close."

"So it's not safe?"

You could never win with my mother—or with Leonard.

"Why is she such a pain?" he complained to me. "She acts like she's from Mars."

"Not Mars, sweetie," I said. "Morrisania, in the Bronx. Which is almost as far from here as Mars, culturally speaking."

CHAPTER 7

Where's the Subway?

While my mother was delighted that I had given her a grandchild in January of 1988, she was as aware of the difference between New York and California as I was. That might explain why it took her so long to make the change. She moved out to California in August of 1989, when Alex was almost two. She found a senior apartment complex a short drive from me, with a kosher meal plan. I thought, great, a built-in babysitter! But Mom spent her first month on the new coast getting sick. First it was the grippe. Then her sciatica acted up. Then she had an attack of gout. I ferried her to doctors and spent more money on babysitters than before she had arrived.

Eventually she settled down, stopped getting sick, and bought a black Ford Taurus. I had another baby, Mike, and my mother got the custom license plate "Bubi 2," for her two grandchildren. She made friends where she lived. She had an air conditioner installed and covered her stacks of unopened boxes with plastic tablecloths to use as side tables. Then a cousin shipped over twenty houseplants from my mom's old Bronx apartment, and my mother was set. She made the twenty-minute drive to visit me twice a week, always commenting on the extraordinary beauty of the highway she used, which ran through a valley in the Santa Cruz Mountain Range and afforded a view eastward toward the Diablo range. I had long since gotten used to the scenery, but my mother marveled at this particular stretch each time she drove it. "I don't know what exactly it is about Highway 280, Preeva," she would say. "Those mountains, they do something to me."

I knew she had adjusted to California completely on October 17, 1989, after the Loma Prieta quake. I called her in a panic to see if she had been hurt in the earthquake that had just broken half the *tchotchkes* in my living room. "Ma, are you all right?" I asked when I finally got through.

"Something like a train rumbled by," she said. "But, Preeva, I thought they didn't have a subway here."

"That was an earthquake, Mom."

"*That* was an earthquake?"

"Yes, a big one, seven on the Richter scale. You were right near the epicenter."

"It really felt like the El train." (That's New York speak for the old "elevated" train.) "It wasn't bad at all. And here all this time I thought earthquakes were a much bigger deal. *Feh.*"

She was one of us now.

It was good to have two moms close by. Helen took my mother under her wing, giving her friendship and some good furniture. Having my mother around relaxed me, so my mother-in-law and I began to get along, too. When I went to the hospital to have child number two, Mike, it was Helen who took care of my older boy, and my mother who came to visit all of them. Both women were happy to speak Yiddish to each other and to share grandparenting duties. To my delight, my kids had something I never had: two living grandmothers. Helen was their *bubbeh* and my mother was their *bubi*. Finally, the difference between Polish and Russian Yiddish pronunciation did me some good—it allowed my kids to have two grandmothers with unique names.

If only both grandmothers had kept their health. I was lacing up my shoes to play a soccer game on a Sunday morning in February 1991 when my mother called to say she wasn't feeling too good. "You *never* feel good, Mom. *How* don't you feel good?" I asked her, thinking of the list of her ailments. By then she was taking pills for heart trouble, high blood pressure, diabetes, and arthritis. Her gall bladder and uterus had been removed in the 1970s. She had smoked for forty years and was carrying one hundred extra pounds. Her upset stomachs came and went mysteriously. She was always depressed, and something was always hurting her.

"Not good," she said. "Come."

Something sounded different. Still wearing my shin guards and shorts, I drove to San Jose and let myself into her apartment. I found her there in bed, sweaty and feverish, and not making much sense. I called her doctor and gave her an analgesic, but after an hour had passed and the Tylenol didn't help, I called an ambulance. Ma was put on a gurney and wheeled downstairs, and I followed.

At the hospital, I waited while the doctors conferred and examined. I called my in-laws, and they came immediately to keep me company. Finally my mother was admitted. They sent her up to a room with an intravenous drip of antibiotics, and I was told I could go home to nurse my baby—Mike was seven months old—and get some sleep.

When I came to the hospital the next day, I learned she had a blood infection, which the doctors assumed had started as a kidney infection and masqueraded as a backache for a month. She had almost died.

"I might have messed up," I told my shrink. "My mom's been talking about wanting to die since my father passed away in 1975. When she finds out she had a chance to go quietly in her sleep, and I screwed it up by getting her to the hospital, she's going to yell at me."

"But she called you," my therapist said. "That shows she really wants to live."

I really wanted her to live, too. And she did, for seven more years, surrounded by her books and knickknacks, making more friends, and seeing her grandchildren every week. When she died, the movers packed up all her stuff and brought it to my house, and I shoved it into the basement—my mother's entire life, reduced to fifteen boxes. It made me sad to look at them.

CHAPTER 8

Zachor, Remember

That stupid billboard along Interstate 580 in Hayward got me every time. When I passed it, an intense despair washed over me. On good days, I'd only have a tear or two. On bad days, I'd have to pull off the highway to cry. The billboard reminded me that people I loved were gone. I would never get them back.

It was a picture of a round orange button that said "easy," and it reminded me of the orange button that stood out against the dark blue collar of my mother's London Fog raincoat. In Hebrew letters, her button said *zachor*, "remember." My mother wore it to remind my father that she understood his pain, even though she was safe in America while he went through one of the worst times in modern history, a time that brutally altered his world. After he died, my mother continued to wear the button; her husband's ice-green gaze had blessed it every day.

I didn't wear any buttons to remember the war. I didn't have to. As a small child, I knew the war had killed the girl on the wall. She was my sister, the one my father loved too much to talk about. I still knew nothing more about her, even though I had lived with her presence every day, her picture hanging where mine should have been. When I began Kinneret day school, facts from the war were drilled into me, even as I pretended not to pay attention—six million Jews, millions of children. The names of concentration camps were added to our Seders, at the point where we let in Elijah.

I was in school when my mother sold those orange buttons in the late 1960s and early 1970s for fifty cents apiece to raise money for Pioneer Women. Most of the survivors of the Holocaust were still alive. They wanted only to have children and lead normal lives, but they themselves weren't normal. People like my parents listened stonily to their children's childish problems and said things like, "Go without food for a week, then you'll know what trouble is."

To me *zachor* meant death and excuses. Growing up, I saw the Holocaust—the war—invoked as an excuse for everything. And I mean *everything*.

It was an excuse not to take outings I wanted: "Mom, why can't we go to Palisades Park?" I asked my mother. "They have rides."

"Your father is tired. He lived through the war."

It was an excuse for the eccentric behavior of my relatives: Whenever my uncle Imi acted crazy, out came the war. "He was a teenager during the war," my mother would say, as if that explained it.

"Mommy, why does Aunt Blanka cry so much?" I asked after my aunt went through three tissues during a one-hour synagogue service, hiding the dirty ones in her sleeve.

"She can't help it, Preeva. It was the war."

"The war" was a constant black cloud, the touchstone of all misfortunes. When my father got cancer, people shook their heads sadly and said, "First the war, now this."

Putting up with survivor parents and their particular set of problems and survivor guilt was enough *zachor* for me. I developed an aversion to learning anything more about those years. As a teenager in the '70s, I rolled my eyes at the frequent mentions of the "six million," and in the early '70s, as a young teen at a movie theater with summer camp friends, I ran out of a screening of the documentary *Night and Fog* in hysterics. I refused to watch the *Holocaust* miniseries on television or read books on the topic. The least little reminder, such as being in a long line at an airport, made me perspire and turned my vision grainy and sepia tinted like an old photograph. When my father died, the injustice of the war he survived and the illness that sank him convinced me to turn my back on all that. No more *zachor* for me. I was busy with college and getting married and raising a family.

Remember? I tried as hard as I could to forget. I did the minimum work of acknowledging the past—one six-week encounter group shortly after I got married with other survivors' children had convinced me that my demons were common among our generation, and that had been that.

But somehow, memory always had ways of finding me. The sadness arose unbidden. While preparing my first Seder, the aroma of the *haroset*—a mixture of apples, walnuts, wine, and cinnamon—threw me back into the times when I helped my mother make this dish with a chopping blade in a wooden bowl. When the rabbi sang the blessings over the wine, I could hear my father instead, and see again my mother's white tablecloth, and the round metal tray she placed beneath the candelabra. When it rained, I smelled the damp wool of my father's winter coat. Over the years, I still tried to avoid Holocaust events, including not participating in the founding of the United States Holocaust Memorial Museum (USHMM), in which my in-laws were active. First they helped to raise money, and I stood aloof, even as I enthusiastically raised money for other Jewish causes. Then they went to Poland to collect artifacts, and all I said was that one of their traveling companions was an alumna of my college. When they paid for their whole family to attend the opening of the USHMM I went, but with my own agenda.

I desperately wanted to find places where my father's world intersected with mine, to find someone like the shoe seller from the Catskills who had remembered the mischievous Adler boys. Every time I met people with an Eastern European accent, I asked them whether they knew Munkach, whether they remembered my father and his brothers. I even had an opportunity to chat with Elie Wiesel, but when he said that, no, he had not known my father's town or family, I turned my back on the Nobel Prize winner and headed for the buffet table.

Years after the museum opened, a dinner was held to reunite the American liberators and the liberated Jews, and I finally took notice. The emcee introduced a man who had escaped the Nazis and joined up with a Russian army unit. He had "played every role possible in the Holocaust: hidden Jew, rescuer, prisoner, and soldier," just like my father. It was the first I'd heard of anyone who had lived a life like the one my father had described. Then the man spoke, and his accent threw me back over the years—the unmistakable sound of Munkach.

I put down my fork as he described a journey to heroism that paralleled my father's in its daring and variety: Trading with the Germans. Creating a shelter for Jews. Hiding in the woods with his family. Getting caught, being separated from his family in a selection at Auschwitz, and joining up with the Russians. I had never known whether to believe my father's stories or accept them as apocryphal, but here was proof that another man had done those things. Why couldn't my father have, too?

But I didn't know where to start looking. My frustration over the great unknowns hanging over me continued to plague me. At any time, I could be overcome by what I called the fullbacks of melancholy, who tackled me into helplessness.

I tried therapist after therapist to deal with the burden of these feelings, these memories that were so vivid I feared they were hallucinations. One therapist recommended attending a therapeutic workshop called Healing the Holocaust. I didn't think of the Holocaust like a sore that would heal with the proper medication, but I signed up anyway.

The full-day workshop was held in a small one-story building in Hamilton Field, a converted airfield in Marin County, ninety minutes from where I lived. Two nautical lamps flanked the entrance, one red and one green. Twenty of us, mostly women in our forties to sixties, sat on folding chairs beneath the fluorescent lights. On a side table sat a pot of coffee, an urn of hot water, and bagels and shmears—the communion food of Jews.

The two facilitators were both children of survivors. The man was imposing—six feet tall, balding, with a white beard and bushy ginger eyebrows. His voice was deep yet gentle. He told us his parents had been from Latvia and Poland, were separated at Auschwitz, and were later reunited in Paris, where he was born. He had a background in theater and an interest in bringing together the two sides in conflicts to help them heal together.

The other facilitator was a petite woman with short, curly, graying hair and a soft voice. Her parents were from Bessarabia, in Belarus, and had both lost spouses and children, gone into hiding, and then escaped. As children, she and her brother constructed elaborate fantasy games of heroism and rescue, and she was now a therapist and recent cancer survivor hoping to help herself heal by running this workshop. She wanted us to open our hearts and minds to other people's experiences and to avoid the "crab in the barrel" syndrome of crawling over each other to compete for the title of "who suffered most."

After the introductions, we did various icebreaking exercises—silly walks, improvising dialogues with ever-changing partners—and gradually moved on to more intense encounters. The day made me realize I had picked up my parents' habit of never trusting an answer, demanding to hear it again and again for endless reassurance. That made sense for someone who had survived the terrible betrayals of wartime, but it wasn't making my life any easier.

Then again, how could we—the children of survivors of such brutality—get comfortable acknowledging our doubts and fears when our parents kept telling us we had nothing to worry about and that everything we had was good?

Attending the Holocaust workshop made me more amenable to looking at the past, but not totally amenable. Shortly after my younger son's bar mitzvah in 2003, my father-in-law showed me something he had received in the mail—an official-looking letter in Polish, printed on heavy paper with a red-and-white seal at the top. "The mayor of Łódź wants the whole family to come for the sixtieth anniversary of the end of the ghetto," he said.

"How did the ghetto end?" I asked.

"With deportation. They're making a special monument to the Jews of Łódź at the train station and dedicating it with a whole program—film, music, speeches, conferences, everything. It should really be something."

"A celebration?" I asked, incredulous.

"Lots of survivors are going. It will be like a reunion. I can't miss this chance. You and Leonard and the boys will come too."

"I don't know," I said. "My father never went back to Munkach."

"So? This is Łódź. Our ghetto was special."

Jack thought it would be a good idea for my sons to see where he used to live: 20 Nova Zazefska. He sat me down when I first married into the family and made me memorize the address, the way you do with children so they won't get lost.

I had many reservations about the trip, but I went along with it. We all flew to Warsaw in August 2004 for a week of Polish Jewish history, followed by three days of Łódź Jewish history in particular. We started in Warsaw and toured the Jewish Historical Institute, and then it was on to the *umshlagplatz*, or "deportation plaza," where the names of every local family put on the trains to the camps was engraved in stone. We walked around the site of the Warsaw Ghetto uprising. Then the twenty-two of us, all somehow related to Jack, jostled politely for the best seats on the private tour bus. Our guide was named Sebastian, but in my mind I called him Christian.

Our itinerary included the towns of Lublin, Cracow, Lagif, and Czestochowa; the camps at Majdanek and Auschwitz; and the final three days of festivities at Łódź. We saw the places where Jews had once lived and died: concentration camps, death camps, *yeshivot*, synagogues, *mikvot*, and cemeteries. "Which Jews wound up here?" I asked the very knowledge-able Sebastian at the preserved camp at Majdanek, which looked like the set from *Hogan's Heroes*. "Mostly the ones from Poland," he said, which probably meant it was no one I knew. My father's family had been from Carpathian Ruthenia and had been deported to camps along with Jews from Hungary. I lost interest in the camp and went outside to look at the flowers.

Throughout the trip, my attention wandered. I didn't feel the personal pull I thought I would, the feeling that this is where my family had been; this is what had happened to me and mine.

I also found my mother-in-law's reactions odd. "Ma, why don't we stop and have a picnic?" I asked when we got to the town where Helen had lived until she was nine. Lagif (also called Lagow or Lagov) was a pretty little place, with a park in the center and trees all in bloom. "Maybe someone who remembers your family will come up and talk to you." We had come this far, after all.

"I'm not interested," she replied curtly.

Finally we got to the extensive complex at Auschwitz—my family's alma mater, so to speak. Here, a local guide joined us after we fed the archivists whatever information we had so they could look up our relatives. I didn't have much to offer, just my father's name, birthday, and town of origin. We waited in a room with a long table for answers.

"Here it is," Jack said, showing us the index card they found for him. "Here's the day I arrived, and the day I went out to the work camp in Ahlem."

I took the guide aside. "Don't you have anything on a Samuel Adler? Anything at all?"

"Not with that birthday," she said. I felt like a barbell had dropped on my stomach.

Because the Jews of Hungary had been processed at Auschwitz, I fell behind the group while I scoured the thousands of photos in the exhibits, searching for an unusually tall man who could be my father, or the high cheekbones of my uncles, or the blonde ringlets of the girl on the wall. All I saw were photos of frightened strangers. At the place where insubordinate prisoners had been shot, I became dizzy and short of breath. My nostrils filled with the smell of blood. I sat down and refused to go on with the tour, waiting instead to get back on the bus.

The next stop wasn't any easier. That was Birkenau, a relatively newer and more menacing camp, where I had heard my own father say he had been. I could not bear to hear what the guide was saying about it, so I took a map and again broke free of the group, heading to one of the barracks. I gazed up at the dusty ceiling. "Daddy, Uncle Imi, Uncle Willy, Aunt Petya, Aunt Batya, I'm here," I whispered. "You escaped. You lived. You had ten children between you, and you had good lives." I didn't add that my father had died early, an uncle had a stroke at fifty-seven, another was manic-depressive, and an aunt had been unstable. They had survived, and they had been mine, at least for a time.

I sat down and cried—for them, for me, for everything. I didn't want to get back on the bus with my husband's family; I wanted the Adler cousins here by my side. After my father died, the cousins had all drifted apart, spreading across the country from Long Island to Oregon. I did not go to their weddings. I had no idea what their children looked like.

I left my tears to dry on the barracks floor. On my way back to the group, I saw that my kids were playing on the train tracks. I started running toward them, intending to scream at them to get off those evil iron rails, but that's when my father-in-law called out: "Time for a group photo! Everyone on the tracks!"

We assembled, as he desired. The four survivors in our group stood in front. I'm the one in the second row on the left who looks very uncomfortable.

Touring Poland with somebody else's family gave me a hunger to arrange such a trip with my own. When I got home, I tried calling a few of my relatives. They all said a reunion of some sort sounded like a great idea, but when it came time to schedule it, everyone was too busy. There seemed to be nothing left of my big, loving family of cousins—nothing but memories.

Extended Tramiel-Gertel-Alpert clan in 2004 (photo by Sara Tramiel)

CHAPTER 9

Heshi on Hershi

As I neared my fiftieth birthday, I decided to look at my past again and reopen my mother's boxes.

They were in the basement, filling nearly two sets of industrial shelving six feet high. Slowly, piece by piece, in the eleven years since my mother's death, I had organized all but one—a blue-and-white Bacardí rum box that was still full of documents and mysteries. I had opened it a couple of times and even had some of its documents translated but never really dealt with the rest.

"Honey, could you turn the extra light on?" I called to my husband, whose home office—a nest of computers, bookcases, and papers—was at the other end of the basement.

I hauled the box off the shelf and sat on the floor with it. At the top were proofs of a set of photos of me from Macy's Photo Club and a couple of old passport pictures of my father. Inside a pretty box that used to hold cherry chocolates were old recipes, pictures of my mother's family, and an envelope from a lawyer's office in Manhattan. The lawyer's envelope held a copy of the invitation to my parents' wedding in the Bronx, and their caterer's bill for $483.

I took a deep breath and plowed ahead. At the very bottom of the Bacardí carton, in a flat paper bag from Caldor's, was an oversized dark brown manila folder. In my father's penmanship it was labeled *Mista-*

Doposi, "assorted documents." Some of these I had already shown to a friend of my father-in-law's, a man from Hungary, to translate—the Hungarian birth, death, and marriage records of my father's first family. These documents upset and confused me. Why did my father's marriage to Suri and the births of their two children, a boy named Bela and the girl on the wall, need so much proof?

Hajmalka in 1943 or 1944

Now I forced myself to look at the documents again, and to think of what they meant. It was a puzzle. I had heard virtually nothing about the boy until after my father was dead, but I had looked at the girl every day in her place of honor above my father's bed. I had heard her name as "Hana," but in these documents it said Hajmalka. *Haj-mal-ka*—what a strange name, stranger even than Preeva. My father must have liked giving his daughters strange names, but what did this one mean? Could it have come from *malka*, the Hebrew word for *queen*? Figures. She gets to be the queen, while I'm fruitful, the breeder.

Hajmalka, my dead rival. That she was dead made her harder to defeat. She never asked for anything. Never complained. Always golden in her gilded frame.

If I knew any Hajmalkas today, I would probably hate them. Instead, sometimes I hate myself. It must be *her* fault. Every time I screw up, I should say, "Hajmalka did this to me."

* * *

As for the boy, Bela, it seemed in retrospect that my father had wanted to erase his memory. No picture of Bela lived on the wall. Years later, my mother had two stories to tell about the dead boy. "When your father went to the ghetto to visit family, the little boy urinated against a wall. Someone saw that he was circumcised, meaning he was a Jew, so they were never allowed to leave the ghetto after that. It was the boy's fault your father wound up in Auschwitz."

And the second story was this: "In the line at Auschwitz, your father was tall and saw that women holding children went to the left, and women who were not holding children went to the right along with the men. So he said to his wife, Suri, 'Give the baby to your mother if you want to live.' That was the boy, not the girl, because he was older but always so sickly. Suri refused to give him to her mother, and she went to the left. Your father never saw any of them again."

The documents in the Bacardí box confused as much as enlightened me. My father's official name on some of them was Samuel Armin. *Armin?* No one I knew ever called him that. He was Hershi, Shmeel Hersh, Shmuel Tzvi, Herman, even Harry, but never Armin.

I could not make out the documents with Cyrillic lettering. Nor did I try to read the Hebrew ones or get translations for the ones that might have been in Czech. I didn't want any more surprises.

"Oh, Len, I miss my Daddy so much," I said as the tears began to spill. I moved the folder away so I wouldn't get the old paper wet. Eventually, I put some of those documents, along with the photos I couldn't identify, into a black, plastic envelope folio. I thought of it as the mystery envelope because it contained so many questions I hoped someday to answer.

I brought out the boxes again hours before my fiftieth birthday party. I had decided to create a slide show to give my West Coast friends an idea of the life I had lived and the family I had come from. Two of my twenty cousins flew in for the party and helped me scan around two hundred photos into my computer at my kitchen table. One of the photos was from my father's time in Israel when he was briefly married to a woman my mother scornfully referred to as "the Romanian." I included the picture because my father looked so handsome in his suit and tie, with the touch of gray at his temples.

After the party, Lottie, one of my husband's cousins, told me she was shocked that my history was so complicated. "And that other family your father had," she said. "What was the first wife's name?"

"Suri," I said.

"And his children? And the second wife?"

My father and Miriam, his second wife

To my shame, I could not remember.

The fullbacks of melancholy were back in force. Maybe it was because I was now fifty, or maybe I was going insane. My therapist at the time thought that my memories plagued me because they existed in isolation from one another, without a coherent narrative to give them context and structure. As an experiment, I brought some of the past back into the light by reframing three of my father's old photographic portraits from Munkach. One was the girl on the wall, Hajmalka. The second was of Hajmalka with her mother and her brother, who was wearing a beret and holding a toy rifle. The third picture was a wedding portrait of Suri in a white satin dress and floor-length veil and my father in formal morning dress, black tails and gray slacks, holding a pair of white gloves. He sits on a stool, Suri's hand on his shoulder.

I still felt that the contrast between Suri's lot and my mother's was unfair. My mother only had a few candid snapshots scattered around until I collected them for her into a little album. Why did my father's first wife and children get fancy gold frames when the frame around my picture came from Woolworth's? There were no pictures at all of my mother in her satin dress and veil. It seemed that my father had taken more pride in his first family than in my mother and me.

After my party in September, I made a concerted effort to seek out people who had known my father. My first major find was Heshi Gorewitz, the same Heshi who had told me my parents were coming to stay at my camp when Hanna the crazy cook was making a goulash of everything. I found him on Facebook, and he was my first stop when I made a trip to New York with a new mission in mind: to fill in some of the blanks of my father's life. Outside the subway at Bainbridge Avenue in the Bronx, a short drive from my father's old shop, I called Heshi's cell phone. "I'm next to a tire place and across from a mattress store," I said. "I'm wearing a purple jacket. Come find me." Heshi picked me up and drove me around the old neighborhood. "I really liked your parents," he told me. "Your mother was something. She really took charge."

"Tell me more," I said. "Was my father easy to get along with? The summer my father was at camp he had cancer. Was he angry all the time?"

"Angry? Not that I recall," Heshi said. "We used to talk for hours."

I was shocked. How could my father, whose life was derailed so often by cruel twists of fate, not be angry about having terminal cancer? When I rode the subway back to Manhattan after visiting Heshi, I realized I was no closer to understanding my father than before.

Hoping for more insight, I rented a car and headed out to visit my cousin Ronit, now a doctor in Dix Hills on Long Island. Since I had last seen her, she had changed her specialty from pain control to cosmetic procedures. Maybe that's why her husband's formerly wrinkled brow was now smooth and shiny as a waxed Formica countertop.

Growing up, I had been jealous of the older Ronit—a tall, blonde, beautiful ballerina. The three-year age difference between us was no longer consequential, although in some ways we were still worlds apart. She wanted to talk politics, for one thing, and we had voted differently in the contentious 2008 presidential election. Also, it was difficult to get her to talk about my father, instead of hers. She finally admitted that her father used to talk a lot about what it was like to kill people.

"Wow, my dad only talked about what it was like to see people die," I said.

Ronit lowered her voice. "You know they were with the Bielski brothers, right?"

"You're kidding!" This was exciting news. Tuvia, Zues, and Asael Bielski had recently been immortalized in a movie depicting how they hid an entire town of Jews from the Germans by building a village in the Byelorussian forest. My father had said he'd hidden Suri and their children in the woods, but I never knew he meant *those* woods.

Or did he? I wanted to hear more, but Ronit either did not remember or did not want to share. Instead, she turned my attention to a photo book, where she lingered over the glossy pages. "This book is all about the Adlers," she said, promisingly. "It shows how they went on to make great lives for themselves. See how beautiful?"

I searched the pages eagerly, hoping to learn something new or see a photo that would spark a synaptic connection, but the pictures were mostly duplicates of what I already had at home.

Then it was back to politics.

The next morning, Ronit headed out to her medical practice and I stayed behind, waiting for the traffic on the Long Island Expressway to die down. I felt glum, but I nodded good morning when Allison, Ronit's youngest, came downstairs.

"Is it true my *zaide* was a partisan?" she asked me shyly.

I looked at her with a slowly growing delight. There was hope for the next generation after all! The first thing I did when I got home was to reward Allison's curiosity by photocopying a batch of documents that mentioned her grandfather. I had the documents translated, and mailed them out in a package to Allison, Imi's granddaughter. I never heard about those documents again, but I know from personal experience that it can take a person half a lifetime to open that Pandora's box.

Back home, I resumed my routines. Singing at Saturday services at Congregation Etz Chayim made me feel like I was back with my parents at the kitchen table in the Bronx. It was also a reminder of how I had failed to engage Leonard in this weekly ritual that was so important to me. One Shabbat it was all too much, and I was in the ladies' room crying about it when I heard someone sobbing in the next stall. I recognized who it was based on the sniffles. "Naomi?" I said. "What's wrong?"

"It's Brian," she said through the partition. "He's in LA instead of being here with me."

"What's he doing in LA?"

"With his mother and sister, celebrating Christmas!" she wailed.

I clucked in sympathy. "I miss my husband, too," I said. "He's turned into a militant atheist."

"Atheist? So is my father, but he was also a Zionist."

As we splashed cold water on our tear-puffed faces at the sink, we discovered something else in common—that Naomi's parents had been in Kibbutz Sasa with my mother in 1950. Before that, her mother had been my mother's friend in the Bronx.

"We heard through the grapevine that your father was a war hero," Naomi's mother said when I visited the family the following week. "Is it true?"

What little girl doesn't think of her father as a hero? "Yes," I said. "Yes, he was."

But was he? I was disturbed by my father's contradictory stories: Passing as a German and trading with the Nazis, yet putting on his *t'fillin* to pray—hiding with his family in the woods, getting sent to Auschwitz, doing things he was ashamed of for a lump of sugar, joining up with a group of Russian soldiers and creating a hiding place for a family of Jews.

I told my father-in-law of my plan to someday reconstruct my father's history. "Why now?" he asked. "Ten years ago, when I told you to see about getting restitution, you didn't want to hear it."

"My father didn't run after restitution when he was alive, so I'm not doing it either," I explained. "It's his history I'm interested in. I mean, why did you take your grandchildren to the Lower East Side?" Jack and Helen had lived in a cold-water walk-up on Second Street right after the war.

"So they could see how we lived," he said.

"Well, there you go," I said. "My father spent nine years of his life in Israel, and I know nothing about it. I didn't even know who some of the people were in the slide show at my party. Not knowing is driving me crazy."

I went to Israel three times before I was twenty-five—twice with my parents when I was a child, another time during college, thirty years ago. Leonard's one trip there had been enough for him. "Too many Israelis in Israel" was his position.

With or without the company of my husband, it was time. When an offer popped up in my in-box for a discounted fare to Israel, I clicked the "book it!" button.

CHAPTER 10

There's No Place like Home

When I clicked on that trip to Israel, it was early 2009. I had not traveled alone for years. Before the children were born in 1988 and 1990, I was always excited to go on a plane. The wonder of flying enchanted me. Always preferring a window seat, I couldn't help but smile as the great engines revved and we went faster and faster and then smoothly lifted off the tarmac. In the 1980s, I used to joke about planes being airborne busses.

Until 1991, when I went to visit my cousin Sam Kahan in Chicago. I thought that the plane trip, when Alex was three and Mike was less than a year old, was something I could handle. That might have been a mistaken assumption, because I was not the best travel agent in the world. On one trip, Leonard and I came to the airport, parked the car, got to the plane, got in our seats, and then discovered, to our embarrassment, we were a day early. On another trip, we drove to the wrong airport—at my direction. Even more embarrassing was the time we were going to watch an eclipse on the Big Island of Hawaii earlier in the year, and I booked our flight into the wrong airport—I didn't know there were two airports on the island—and we had to rent a car and drive an hour and a half to get to the right place to meet our group. I had trouble with time zones, too. When I was visiting New York, I would call people in California before dawn. When I was in California, I would make birthday calls to Israel on the wrong day of the week.

But I persisted in traveling, even alone with the children, who were pretty good travelers. They enjoyed the games I packed for them, and the older one thought nothing of walking up and down the aisles of the plane looking for playmates. So I planned the trip to Chicago to visit my favorite cousin, Sam Kahan, twelve years my senior and married to a woman who had declared me her sister. Sam had bounced me on his knee when I was born and lived in a family-friendly area of West Rogers Park. The trip to Chicago went well, even traveling with two children by myself, and it imbued me with a combination of cockiness and idiocy.

* * *

Then the day for going home arrived. Alex, Mike, and I had been having a leisurely breakfast at my cousin's house, believing we had plenty of time to catch our one thirty flight. Then someone asked, around ten o'clock, when my flight back home was.

"I think it's one thirty, let me see."

I checked my ticket and saw a lot of numbers and letters that had no meaning to me. I asked my cousin, who traveled on business all the time, to read my ticket.

"Uh, oh, *bubbeleh*," he told me, "your plane is at eleven thirty."

"Oh, no, what do I do?"

"It's okay. Don't panic. I do this all the time."

I believed him. Like a well-oiled machine, his wife and children loaded the car and strapped my children into their car seats before I had my shoes on; Sam went over the directions and wrote them down for me.

Following his directions, I drove fast around the local streets of Chicago, almost ran several stop signs, hastily handed the guy at the curb-side check-in my rental car keys and twenty bucks and asked him to return the car for me, and ran like hell for the gate. I was pushing a stroller with a three-year-old, carrying a baby in a frame pack on my back, and juggling a diaper bag, a booster seat, and a four-foot-tall stuffed Batman. I was running so fast that, while I knew that murals covered the walls, I could not tell what they depicted.

It was going to be close.

As I got to the gate I heard someone say there were still three empty seats! My seats were there!

I ran up to the gate agent and gave her my tickets "Your ticket for this flight isn't here," she said.

"What are all those papers?"

"This is the receipt for your flight from San Jose to Chicago and your receipt for your flight to San Jose from Chicago. The flight coupon from Chicago to San Jose is missing."

"Can I buy a new ticket?"

"Not in time to get on the plane, sorry," and the agent closed the door to the Jetway.

I called Leonard at work from a pay phone.

"Hello?" he said.

"Honey, I missed the plane." And I started to cry.

"Mommy, what's wrong?" Alex said at my hip.

"Mommy's sad because we missed our plane. It's okay."

"What?"

"I'm crying, Len. Alex wants to know why."

"Why are you crying?"

"I ran so fast!" I blubbered. "Alex and Mike were so good, they cooperated so well, we ran, and I did *everything*. I gave the curbside check-in guy the keys like your dad told me, and the door was open, and there were three seats left—those were our seats—and my ticket was missing! And they closed the door to the plane."

"Ticket missing? And you didn't notice?"

"You know plane tickets confuse me. I never know what I'm looking at."

There was a moment of silence. With all the embarrassment, extra trips to the airport, and extra driving, I had never actually *missed* a plane. And I had missed it because I had lost my ticket, the stupidest thing I could ever imagine doing.

That humiliation stung for sixteen years. Because Leonard had not wanted to go, I declined invitations to go to Israel, France, and New York with other family members. Because Leonard had not wanted to go, I even missed Joe Salsberg's last hurrah, a testimonial dinner in Toronto that everyone knew would be his last. I had really wanted to see that.

But I decided to go to Israel on my own. All I was carrying this time was a bundle of questions about my father's story.

CHAPTER 11

Jabotinsky Bridge

Israel is a country of archives and museums. I had been making connections there through two online forums and mailing lists for alumni and friends of Zionist youth movements. One was called Shomernet, for alumni and friends of Hashomer Hatzair, the youth movement my mother belonged to. The other one was Habonet, created for the alumni and friends of Habonim. A considerable overlap existed between the groups, both created to support leftward-leaning, labor-friendly youth movements, both comprised of people who lived around the world, though most lived in the United States and Israel. I talked myself into believing that my mystery folder's contents could easily be deciphered and decoded once I was overseas, especially with all the connections I had made.

On my first full day in Tel Aviv, I went looking for 38 King George Street, home of the Jabotinsky Archives that contained the history of Betar, my father's youth movement.

Ze'ev Jabotinsky was the biggest hero of my father's youth. He was born in Poland, but the movement he started spread across Europe and the world. Betar advocated for a new kind of Jew, one who was not afraid to use physical force and who would care for his fellow Jews while standing proud among the non-Jews of the world. Betar imagined a Jewish state that stretched from the Mediterranean Sea to the Indus River. When the British partitioned the Middle East into Arab and Jewish lands, the Betar people were opposed to accepting the proposed borders. They did not want to retreat to the Jordan River, since this created a tactically vulnerable state. Betaris wanted Transjordan, as well.

Their views got them expelled from the Zionist Congress, but the movement thrived nevertheless and swept up thousands of young people, including my father. Dad had boasted of being the great man's driver when Jabotinsky toured Carpathian Ruthenia in the early 1930s.

I had always wondered about Jabotinsky and his bridges. Every time my family took a trip in the car, it was as if Jabotinsky were sitting right there in the front seat between my parents. My mother and father, like the farmer and the cowboy in Oklahoma, liked to get in digs at each other, so every time we passed a short bridge, my mother pointed and said, "Look, Gesher Jabotinsky!" That meant a short bridge that went nowhere. Jabotinsky was not a tall man.

An entire institute is dedicated to Jabotinsky in Tel Aviv, and that was my first stop. I had e-mailed the staff of the Jabotinsky Archives in advance of my arrival, certain that they could help me find out more about my father. I found the address on King George Street, in an old neighborhood where the palm trees had outgrown the structures. A smell of fish cooking permeated the air. The museum took up half a block in a stucco building three stories tall. I told the receptionist that I had an appointment with an archivist and began to tell her some of my tale in English and broken Hebrew. "My father was a Betarnik from Munkach," I began.

The receptionist nodded excitedly and said in Hebrew, "Yes, yes, my mother is from Munkach too!"

I felt I was in the right place.

A tall woman came through the doorway and extended her hand. "I am Olga, the librarian," she said in perfect English and a heavy Russian accent. "You are looking for records on Adler Hershi, also known as Hershi Adler, correct?"

"He was Jabotinsky's driver in the thirties," I said, sounding important.

Olga gave me a professional smile, as if everyone who came through the door claimed to be Jabotinsky's personal driver, personal hairdresser, and personal dog walker. She showed me to a room with long wooden tables that had built-in keyboards and monitors. "You can access the archives in here," she said and left me.

I placed my folder on the table and began by typing in Samuel Adler. Nothing.

Then I searched for Hershi Adler.

Nothing.

I searched for Munkach and found a few pictures of Jabotinsky at a banquet, no driver in sight.

I tried just Adler. There were plenty of those, mostly from Poland, but the database had no record of a Samuel Adler or a Hershi Adler. I tried every combination and permutation I could think of, including the names of his brothers and parents, but nothing came up.

Reluctantly, I went to find Olga at her desk just outside the library. "There must be some mistake," I told her. "I can't find my father."

She gave me a practiced smile of condolence, like an undertaker. "Many people come here searching," she said. "Not all of them find what they are looking for."

"Is there anywhere else I can check?"

Even Olga's sigh seemed to have a Russian accent. She accompanied me back to the table and showed me how to access photographs of the area around Munkach. I spent the next few hours searching for my father's face in the crowds that surrounded Jabotinsky and other people from the Betar movement in that part of the world, in that time period—page after page of scanned photos, my nose practically touching the screen.

I was racing through the photos quickly by now, but I flipped back to one that showed a line of young people raising a flag in a clearing in a forest. They were saluting as one of them played a bugle. One of the men in the picture was tall. My father had been tall. I marked it.

There was another photo from that day, a group photo with eight girls and ten boys. I thought that one of the boys looked sort of like my father, a family resemblance. There was another photo, of Jabotinsky walking through a town square followed by a tall man with an earnest face and strong jaw. I marked that one, too, and did some arithmetic. These pictures were taken in 1935. My father was born in 1911 and would have been the right age to reach maturity and grow strong along with the movement Jabotinsky began in 1923.

I called Olga over to see. Again, she gave me the undertaker look. "One photo can look a lot like another," she said. She pointed out that the tall men in the pictures seemed too old for a youth of twenty-four.

I made copies of the three photos anyway. Olga gave me a receipt for the two dollars it cost to use the printer and wished me well.

On my way out, I passed an exhibit on the illegal smuggling of Jews to Israel and paused to scan through the ship manifests for my father's name, but it seemed I had made a long, expensive trip for nothing.

Destination number two, the Etzel Museum, was housed in the basement of the building, and dedicated, not surprisingly, to The Etzel, a branch of fighters who chose to pursue Jabotinsky's vision of a free Israel by blowing up institutions of the British Mandate. My father's risk-taking personality had naturally led him to serve in the Etzel; perhaps I would find a mention of him here. It was an underground army whose soldiers led two lives: bowing and scraping to the British Mandatory government of Palestine, while at the same time plotting to blow up their places of work.

History had mostly not been kind to these men. When they blew up the Acco Prison, for example, they were hailed as heroes, but when they blew up the King David Hotel, mainstream Zionists denounced them. Relations between the Etzel and the more moderate military group, the *Haganah*, worsened to the point where their two groups had fired on each other off the shores of Tel Aviv. This incident, the Altalena affair, has become shorthand for internecine warfare between different factions of Zionists that happened around the founding of the State of Israel. The group's most famous alumnus, Menachem Begin, took charge of the Altalena and eventually surrendered to the *Haganah*.

What greeted me first, in silver letters two feet high, was the commandment to remember: *yizkor*, the infinitive of *zachor*. Beyond that was a collection of dusty cases containing samples of Bren guns and dioramas of the group's infamous "operations," including one where they blew up the Haifa Police Station from the inside and stole a bunch of arms. From stories my father had told, I wondered whether he had been part of this operation, but there was no mention of my father's name. Again, the trail turned cold.

I kept trying. I visited the museum of the Haganah housed in a Bauhaus building in Tel Aviv in a very fashionable neighborhood. Here, the air conditioning was better and the exhibits easier to navigate. Several young Israeli soldiers stood guard and took tickets. I hung around the lobby, unsure how to proceed, my father's picture dangling from my hand as people came and went. Finally, I stopped the oldest man I saw. I could tell by his bearing that he was ex-military.

"Excuse me, sir?" I said in my bad Hebrew. "I'm here from California, researching my father's life from the war years before I was born. He fought in the War of Independence. Could you look at this picture and tell me if you knew him?"

The old man looked closely, his brow furrowed. Twice, he almost said something, but in the end he shook his head. "Sorry, I do not recognize him," he said in English. "The archives are right through that door. Go, and someone will help you."

I went. It was a library, its high walls lined with books. There was a table in the center and great big windows open to catch every breeze. A black-and-white cat ambled in, which I took as a good sign. I love cats.

Tucked into one corner of the long, high-ceilinged room was a desk with a computer—and a librarian, Doreit Hermann. I told her of my quest.

"Ms. Hermann," I said, "my father's name was Shmuel Tzvi Adler, and he died when I was young, too young to do more than hear stories from him." I brought out my folder of documents. "I am trying to find out if his stories were true and to fill in his locations between 1946, when he was in Prague, and August 1948, which is what I have on his Histadrut card." He had told me that on one Rosh Hashanah during that time, he and his brothers went up on a roof to do Tashlich because there had been gunfire in the streets. I wanted to pin down what year that had happened. There had been war in the streets of Israel for years. Was this story from 1946, 1947, or 1948?

The woman typed something into her computer. "Yes," she said.

"What do you mean, 'yes'?"

"I found him."

"You *found* him?" I bounced up and down on my formerly tired feet.

"He has a service record," said Doreit.

"Let me see!"

"Sorry, these records aren't public; they are not just for your father," said Doreit. "But his mother's maiden name was Weiss?"

"Yes, yes! Weiss! Can you tell me anything else?" I craned my neck to see her monitor, even though I don't read Hebrew very well. Doreit frowned and turned the monitor away from me.

"No, I can't tell you anything about what I see here, except that he arrived in Palestine in 1947."

This by itself was a revelation. The last documentation I had for my father was Prague, 1946, when he applied for a driver's license.

When, exactly, did he arrive in Palestine? His police identification card placed him in Haifa in 1948. So now I had a new bit of information about his whereabouts but no details. What had my father done in Prague before 1947, and how had he gotten into a land where Jewish immigration was strictly controlled? Had he entered the country legally, or did he swim ashore under cover of darkness? What ship had he taken to Palestine? Even the smallest progress made me more frustrated.

I trudged over to meet my friend Eti for dinner. One of the reasons I'd had the nerve to get on a plane by myself in the first place was people like Eti, an old high school friend with whom I reconnected through Classmates.com after thirty years. Eti was born Ethel Mlinarski. Her mother, a Bessarabian, had fled her town and hidden from the Germans in the woods. Eti encouraged me to come to Israel and gave me tips on where to stay and how to plan my itinerary. Through her and others, I felt as if I were part of a protective network that would keep me safe and on track.

"How did it go today?" she asked, all bubbly, when I kissed her hello at the Italian restaurant she had recommended.

"Dismal," I replied.

"Aw, Preev. Don't give up."

We ordered pasta and cava, a light fizzy wine from Spain.

"Being survivors' children is quite a burden," Eti said quietly. "We know things other people don't. My mother told me that starvation is the worst way to die and that suicide is preferable to dying of hunger. She also told me that you have to be smart about how you commit suicide." Her mother had witnessed one girl die from eating poisoned mushrooms and had said that it had been worse than starvation. "But slitting your wrists and bleeding to death, now that was pretty peaceful," said Eti. "That was Mom's advice to me."

"Yeah, my father told me what happens when you drink methanol," I said. "After the liberation, he joined the Russian army. He was on a campaign march across Europe with a bunch of Russian troops, and they found a factory with barrels of alcohol. Some of them drank it, thinking it was ethanol, like in liquor, but it was methanol, wood alcohol—poison. The soldiers who drank it went blind, turned blue, and died."

"See all the special things you learn by being the children of survivors?" Eti said.

"To survivors," I toasted.

"To survivors."

We clinked our glasses and drank.

CHAPTER 12

Showdown by the Washing Machine

My next stop was Haifa, to reconnect with my two first cousins who were the daughters of my uncle Ludwig. To get there from Tel Aviv, I rented a car. This surprised my friends when I told them because many Americans are afraid to drive in Israel. Israeli drivers swerve at random, change lanes without signaling, accelerate madly or decelerate without warning, let you into traffic circles or not on a whim, park on the sidewalk, back up for no reason, and always honk their horns. They were my kind of people. After all, I was the daughter of Jabotinsky's driver.

I had not seen my cousin Ditza in thirty years, not since 1978, when I was in college and she was a student teacher. She greeted me at her door as if we were twins separated at birth. "Preevaah!" Her familiar voice and accent enveloped me like a bear hug. She led me into the great room that ran the length of the apartment and said to everybody—her husband, Eli; her sister, Erela, and husband, Gal; Ditza's daughters, Ofri and Gal, and their significant others, Tal and Roy; her niece Eshkar and her husband and their three daughters, Yaari, Mapal, and Agat; and their dog—"Preeva is here!" as if she had waited thirty years for precisely this moment. I had a hard time keeping everyone straight because of the strangeness of the Hebrew names and the two Gals and the Tal, but after the greetings were done and I had at least a weak grasp on the names, I brought out a packet of pictures from my mystery folder. These pictures were not really mysteries, just pictures my mother had taken in 1964 and 1968 when we visited as a family, and my own pictures from 1978. I tried to take a few new pictures of the group, but the light was bad. All during the conversation, I looked for a polite way to ask after my uncle Ludwig's papers. The occasion never came.

I had forgotten that this group of cousins was not a reflective bunch. Ditza and her sister, Erela, five and ten years older than I, respectively, were completely wrapped up in their daily lives: their plans, their families, and their next meal. They had not inherited the "keep in touch" gene from their father, my uncle Ludwig, who never let a year go by without sending at least a blue aerogramme wishing me a happy Rosh Hashanah. The last year of his life, at his request, I had been helping Ludwig each month by wiring money to his bank account.

Ditza's entire family, even the dog, greeted me warmly. "My father loved your father so much," Ditza said, "that when he was very old, he called everyone who was good to him Hershi."

"What else did he tell you about my dad?" I asked eagerly.

"First, we eat!" she said.

Thereafter it was chitchat. Ditza had gone from being a teacher to an official in the Israeli Ministry of Education who set curriculum for preschool teachers. When I tried to switch the conversation back to my father or to her father's old papers, she waved me off.

"Come with me," she said, and I got very excited, but the picture she showed me on a wall in her bedroom was the same one of my grandparents that my father had passed on to me.

"Yes, I have that one. I think we all do," I said. "Didn't you find a family tree in your father's apartment?"

My cousin Sam had told me of an illuminated family tree of the Spinka clan, and I was eager to see it.

"Ach, we haven't gone through his papers yet. It's too painful and I've been too busy. It's only a year since he left us. But tell me about your trip. Do you have any clothes to wash? I can throw them in the machine."

I brought out my dirty jeans and followed my cousin into her laundry room. "Ditza," I said. I was having trouble getting the words out.

"Preeva, what is it?"

"I didn't sit on a plane for fourteen hours and drive here from Tel Aviv for you to do my laundry. Why can't you just sit down and talk to me about my father?"

Ditza measured out detergent into a cup. "I hate talking about my American uncles," she said. "Whenever one of my father's brothers came to visit, we always had to meet them at the airport with red roses and a sign and hug them and kiss them and make a fuss."

"You didn't want to give your uncles a hug?"

She whirled to face me. "You don't understand," she said. "They were so mean to us! And my father was a different person when his brothers were around, crazy and nervous the whole time. I hated those visits."

"Hey, your father had the last laugh," I said. "He not only escaped the concentration camps, he outlived them all."

Ludwig had had the good sense to move to Palestine before 1944.

My cousin's face turned red. I couldn't tell if it was from shame or anger. "But he was only a civil servant," she remonstrated. "He didn't have the money his brothers did and had to depend on them for help."

That was true. According to my mother, my father sent a container of machine tools ahead from Prague to Palestine in 1947, intending to start a new business there. My uncle Ludwig sold the contents of the container— my father's entire nest egg—and kept the money for himself. My father, who was staying with Ludwig, took to his bed for two weeks. Even so, the brothers in America chipped in fifteen years later so that Ludwig could buy an apartment. My father had invited them all to dinner and laid down the law. Brothers help each other, he said. And they had.

"His brothers made him feel terrible," Ditza continued. "Imi used to say to him, 'You abandoned our parents!'"

"Ditza," I said. "I have to tell you that Imi was not right in the head." I took a deep breath and told her about one incident my mother never forgave (to be fair, there were many things my mother never forgot or forgave). Imi had come to visit my father in the hospital and cursed him for getting sick.

"You know why Imi kept visiting Israel?" Ditza said. "He kept a mistress here." I wasn't surprised. My uncle Imi was said to have had many mistresses on the side. "And on one of his trips, he borrowed our blue hatchback and wrecked it. We couldn't afford to fix that car for months." She slammed the machine door shut and pounded the on button.

"But I'm here now, Ditza, trying to figure something out about my father. Not about Imi. About *my* father, Hershi. And whether you like it or not, I know the uncles helped your father buy his first apartment," I added. "I'm sorry about your car, but you shouldn't take what Imi said seriously. He was definitely bipolar, and that caused a lot of trouble. He caused trouble, and he got trouble. It was terrible what happened." I reminded her of what became of our guilt-inducing, car-wrecking uncle. His older son died in 1979, shot to death at his place of business. His younger son died in 1987, victim of a car accident. I couldn't invite Imi to my wedding because his wife had taken out a restraining order on him.

"Look at me, Ditza," I said. "Your father died in 2008. Mine died when I was sixteen, in 1975. I'm sorry to say it, but you probably know more about my father than I do. I want to hear your stories."

Ditza softened. "Come, sit," she said. "We'll have a cup of tea."

At the table, I brought out my mystery folder. I showed her the picture with the woman I could not identify. "Do you know who this is?" I asked her.

She took out her gold-rimmed reading glasses and balanced them on her nose. She studied the photo.

"Yes, I know that woman," she said. "That's Miriam."

"You mean his cousin Miriam? The one from Kibbutz Yasur?"

"No," she said. "Miriam, your father's second wife."

"Oh my God!" I grabbed the photo and examined it more closely. The woman was pretty, with a sharp nose, her hair elaborately curled and swept back off her face. She had a cool smile like a model. I had the court paper from their divorce settlement, but it hadn't mentioned her name.

"My father stayed friends with her after the divorce," Ditza said carelessly.

"What?" I said. "Then you *know* her!"

"I saw her from time to time, but I didn't *know* her."

"Come on, do you remember anything about her?" I asked.

"Hmm," said Ditza. "She was a teacher and very beautiful. That's all I remember. My father loved beautiful women," she added, and we both knew what she meant. Ludwig's wife, Ditza's mother, had been a wonderful woman, sweet and wise and accomplished, a doctor of language, a school principal, and interpreter for the government, but she was homely.

I took notes on what Ditza told me and then showed her another photo, placing it on the table between us.

It was the girl on the wall, my dead sister. I wanted to know whether my cousin had heard anything about her.

Ditza peered at the photo through her glasses. "Isn't that you?" she asked.

I gave a snort. "Do I have blonde hair?" I said. "No, that is not I. Her name was Hajmalka. She was the daughter of Suri, my father's first wife. She's my sister, I guess. But tell me this, why did my father keep her picture over his bed instead of mine?"

"I don't know," Ditza said. "I had a sister who died too, and they kept her photo up. They never wanted to talk about it. These things happened a lot, especially back then."

"I understand that babies don't always live, even without a war going on," I said. "But why didn't they try to deal with these things instead of making us crazy?"

"Who knows? And even if they had told you, all the Adlers were storytellers. To hear them tell it, the State of Israel wouldn't exist without them. You couldn't believe a word they said."

I was quiet for a moment and thought, you were listening to the wrong Adler.

* * *

Despite our confrontation at the washing machine, Ditza invited me to stay with her for the night, because the next day I had to leave early to drive to Jerusalem to visit Yad Vashem, the largest center of Holocaust research and memory in the world. Yad Vashem is more than a museum— it's a monument, an education center, and a social service organization. It keeps track of righteous gentiles, non-Jews who saved lives, especially Jewish lives, during the war. It hosts events to reunite survivors and offers tissues by the entry gates, just after the metal detectors.

I had arranged to meet two people there. One was Sandy Kaufman Bloom, an American cousin from my mother's side who moved to Israel after her marriage in 1977. We kept in touch over the years, and she had come with her daughter and her husband to California in 2001 for my son Alex's bar mitzvah. Sandy worked as a librarian and translator, and she freelanced for Yad Vashem.

I also had an appointment with Zvi Bernhardt, an archivist and historian who was very involved with Yad Vashem's latest project, putting Holocaust information databases online. He was also, coincidentally, a cousin of one of my best friends in California, Jess. Jess had urged me to look at my father's files again and someday visit Yad Vashem.

"What would be the use?" I asked her. "My dad is dead, the last of his brothers is gone, and all of his stories happened in another lifetime, thousands of miles away."

"What, not look?" she said. "Are you crazy? You've got to look!"

"Yeah, but . . ."

"Preeva, those records are a gold mine."

"Yeah, but . . ."

"You have got to go see what else you can find," said Jess. "And, you've got Zvi."

"Who's Zvi?"

"My cousin in Israel. He's the son of my uncle the psychologist, and he's like all of us Bernhardts—very focused, very capable—which is great, since he works in Yad Vashem's electronic archive department."

I met Sandy in the parking garage. Together we went upstairs to meet Zvi in the research room. The nice woman who gave us keys to store our knapsacks in lockers overheard me using the word *Holocaust*, and took me to task.

"The word *holocaust* is from the Greek, meaning 'sacrifice,' which implies willing cooperation," she corrected me in a French accent. "We Jews did not sacrifice anything. We were murdered."

"Um, okay," I said. "So what should I call it?"

"The *Shoah*."

In the research library, Zvi shook my hand. I could tell from his body language that he was eager to sit me down at one of the terminals and leave me there. This library, like the one at the Jabotinsky Archives, had no visible books. Instead, the room was filled with long tables, computer screens, and windows. If you wanted a book, you had to write down a number and have the material retrieved from the stacks.

I took out my mystery folder and said, "I wonder if you could take a look at this, some original documents from my father. They're in a bunch of languages I don't understand."

"Original Documents?" he said, pronouncing each word as if he were capitalizing the *O* and the *D*. He peered at the contents of my folder and his attitude changed. "Come with me to my office."

We took the elevator to an upper floor office crammed with book-shelves stuffed with the journals, photocopies, and extracts that are the lifeblood of an archivist. Stacks of papers teetered, threatening to fall over at any moment, but Zvi knew where everything was, reaching effortlessly for what he needed. He transferred some piles of paper from a small round conference table to the windowsill, thus partly blocking his view of the Jerusalem neighborhood of Har Nof. I spread my own papers on the newly cleared space and explained my puzzlement over them. "For instance, here is a marriage certificate for my father and his first wife," I said, pointing, "while this one over here looks like the same thing, only in a different language."

"Preeva, where on earth did you get all these?" Zvi asked.

"My basement. My mother saved them in a Bacardí Rum box."

He looked at the top sheet and jotted some notes. "Samuel Adler, place of birth Munkach, date of birth June 17, 1911," he muttered. "Let's see what comes up." He woke his computer from sleep and entered some information.

"Hmm," he said. "Who is Abraham Adler?"

"That's my uncle Imi," I said, excited. "Did you find something?"

"I have a record of a Samuel Adler that is linked to that of Abraham Adler. They have consecutive numbers." He was referring to the tattooed number most concentration camp survivors got when they became the chattel of the Germans in the concentration camps. "Your father went first."

That was just like my dad, to go first and show his younger brother what to expect.

"Here it is, Samuel Adler," Zvi said. "Number: 6433."

Oh, my God, 6433. In the office at Yad Vashem, I was overtaken by feelings; I suddenly found myself back in Yonkers, 1975, at my mother's kitchen table.

I had forgotten my father's number, but hearing the digits again brought their story back. Many survivors attached mystical significance to their numbers, and my father had decided that his number corresponded to the years of his marriages: The numeral six was the number of years he was married to his first wife, Suri. The numeral four was the number of years he was married to his second wife, whose name I now knew was Miriam. After he was married to my mother for four years, he concluded that the last two digits went together, and that he would be married to her for a total of thirty-three years. He died sixteen years short of that milestone. "What happened to my thirty-three years?" my mother used to cry, her arms folded on the table. I used to look at her and roll my eyes then. Now I was sorry I had been so cruel to her.

The number 6433 wasn't the only data Zvi Bernhardt found in his computer database. He pulled up a reproduction of an index card with information my father had dictated to a representative of the United Nations Relief and Rehabilitation Administration, a wartime relief organization long gone. It was a summary of the damage suffered at the hands of his captors and listed his days of forced labor, his dates in Auschwitz, his dates at the concentration camp Jaworzno, and the date of his escape from a death march in February of 1945, which is how he and his brother took their leave of the Nazis. The last entry on the card was for 1946, when he filed the report.

It was good that Sandy took great notes because lost in memory, I hardly took in another word after hearing my father's number. Zvi summoned a librarian who knew some Russian and Czech, and between them they managed to get a rough translation of my documents: birth certificates in Hungarian, Czech, and Russian for the children of my father's first marriage; a form in Czech that attested to his status as a survivor of the concentration camps; another in Hungarian that said he worked in Munkach as a chauffeur; and an affidavit in Czech that he was a trustworthy man and a mechanic.

"Hey, look," Sandy said. "One paper says *chauffeur*, and another says *mechanic*. Which one is right?"

"He could have done both," said the translator. "People downplayed their professions to avoid taxes."

It turned out that my father could have chosen among several nations for citizenship. He chose Czechoslovakia. "You could take these documents to the Czech embassy and get EU citizenship for yourself and your children," Zvi told me. "My friend did that, and his son got free college tuition."

"Uh-huh," I said. My head was still spinning.

"Now I want you to do something for me," said Zvi. He handed me some forms to complete. "Please do one each for your brother and sister and for anyone else you can think of who was lost in the Shoah." The papers were blank Pages of Testimony.

For years, since the 1970s, Yad Vashem had been compiling interviews with survivors and others to collect the actual names of the six million Jews who had been lost. The institution is aiming to have a Page of Testimony for each one of the Jews lost in the Shoah, which would be posted to the World Wide Web and shared with the whole world in a massive, searchable database. I had been trying to do this simple task for years but could never finish, always breaking down in tears. Now I was finally filling out the forms for these ghosts of my past at Yad Vashem itself. I had brought individual pictures of Bela and Hajmalka, the brother and sister I had never known. With Sandy's encouragement and support, I finished the task and handed the forms in at the research desk. Once I gave them a place in Yad Vashem's registry, they would live again, forever, on the Internet. With Sandy beside me, and the view through the window of Jerusalem's hills, I managed to complete the task I had been attempting without success for twelve years. I gave my half-siblings eternal electronic life.

When I filled out those forms at the request of Zvi Bernhardt in 2009, there were two million Pages of Testimony. Two years later it was up to four million, distilled from six million entries submitted all around the world.

The list is still growing.

Suri Kahan Adler and her children, Bela and Hajmalka

CHAPTER 13

What My Mother Saw

The fact-finding trip for my father's past gave me just as much insight into my mother, Chaya Zlate Kaufman Adler. I thought that, because we were very close, I knew everything about her. But I never fully appreciated her until I visited the kibbutz where she went to live for three years when she was in her late twenties.

In my childhood in the Bronx, I felt smothered by her. With my father off working six days a week, it was mostly the two of us, alone together in the two-bedroom apartment. I woke to the sound of her rustling the newspaper at the kitchen table, her large frame blocking the path to the refrigerator. Her cup of Sanka always had a spoon in it "to keep the glass from breaking." She talked to herself as she read her three papers, the *Post*, the *News*, and the *New York Times*, so she could get all three political points of view and draw her own conclusions. She always focused on news about urban renewal and other government projects she did not care for. She always suspected graft or, worse, baseless ego as the reason for Robert Moses and his ruination of the Bronx. "That's what people are like today," she groused. "Hooray for me and screw you."

She could smell hypocrisy like a bloodhound. With great sarcasm, she described anyone as "a real up-front guy" if she felt he was hiding a personal agenda behind a façade of bonhomie. Insurance salesmen fell into this category. So did salesmen of penny stocks, mutual funds, corporate bonds, investment pools, and any get-rich-quick scheme—to all of which she felt her husband was uniquely vulnerable. "Anyone can buy your father with a good word," she said, shaking her head.

One of her deepest held grudges was against my uncle Imi, who she said had dissolved a three-way partnership with my father and my uncle Willy. "He threw your father out of the business with a wife and a two-year-old at home," she said. "He claimed your father was too old to have another child."

That must have really bothered her. I was the apple of her eye, but to my uncle I was just another mouth to feed, an only child born to a father who was so old that his own brothers had kicked him out.

I see now that the girl on the wall had been on my mother's mind, too. She treated me as if I might suddenly disappear. Even when she was totally occupied, a cigarette in one hand and a book in the other, she wouldn't let me out of her sight. Terrible things could happen to me while I was in my bedroom working on a crafts project. "Preeva!" she yelled every half hour, panic in her voice.

"WhAAAaT!" I yelled back.

"Okay, just wondering where you were."

Where would I be? I couldn't go anywhere without her permission, even one floor up to see Butchie Bisgaier's aquarium. On the rare occasions when she allowed me to go outside, my territory was restricted to the playground bordered by a privet hedge at the foot of our building. I learned to immerse myself in what was available indoors: paint by numbers, coloring books, records I listened to over and over. "You never nursed when you were a baby," my mother said by strange way of explanation for all her rules and restrictions. "You gave yourself gingivitis twice by putting something in your mouth you shouldn't. You shared your lollipop with a puppy. I can't trust you alone." I was too fast, too wild, so she put me in a harness, keeping me on a leash to control me.

Another way of controlling me was to watch carefully to see what I liked so she could withhold it when I misbehaved. That, I believe, is how I lost Sam Katz, an orange tomcat with the personality of a hunter. He hunted the roast chicken off our kitchen counter. He hunted dishes off the table and broke them. My mother said Sam Katz had to go and treated me to a laundry list of the cat's sins—which sounded suspiciously like many of mine. Can't control him. Can't trust him.

Without Sam Katz, there was really no one to play with. I had never left my mother's side. I was afraid of the bigger kids in the playground, and in any case, I didn't play well with others. My first day of prekindergarten at Jacob Schiff Jewish Community Center, I wouldn't let my mother leave. I grabbed her skirt and further attached myself to it by biting hard on the material. A kindly teacher named Deena took us to a nearby meeting room with a splintery parquet floor that smelled of overheated wood.

"Preeva, it's time to let your mother go," she said. "Will you do that?"

"Noooo," I howled, thus allowing my mother to snatch her skirt out of my teeth. That year I came down with a lot of strep-throat infections and managed to stay home from school as many days as I went.

Later, I began to understand that she had put up with a lot in her marriage, also. After my father died, she told me that he had never stopped talking about his first wife. She only let him hang Hajmalka's picture so that he wouldn't hang his wedding portrait with Suri. That was why I grew up with the girl on the wall staring down at me, refusing to blink. That was my father's version of a compromise.

At Yad Vashem, my cousin Sandy suggested that I try another search for Suri, using the spelling for her maiden name that I found on the Hungarian version of my father's marriage record.

"It won't work," I said. "I already tried from home."

"Try again," she urged me. "You get access to different databases here."

I typed in Sarolta Kahan, and up came a record—a copy of a Page of Testimony on her behalf, written in Hebrew in the 1980s. "She was married to Hersh," Sandy translated for me. There was no mention of any children. "It was filled out by Suri's brother, from an address in Kiryat Motzkin. Someone named Yisrael Kahan."

"Yisrael," I murmured. "Sandy, what would a Hungarian Jew living in Israel with that name actually call himself?"

"A Polish Jew would call himself Srulik," she said. "A Hungarian Jew would say Shragai."

"Are you sure? Shragai?" I knew someone with that name—a man who lived in a funny house, on pillars, with a fishpond built in the shade underneath. I had visited him with my parents on our trips to Israel in 1964 and 1968. Could this man I met actually be Suri's brother?

Suddenly, my respect for my mother tripled. She had heard my father talk endlessly of another woman he had worshiped. Allowed him to put a picture of the woman's daughter on the wall where her own daughter should have been. Had traveled to Israel and broken bread with the woman's brother. I wondered if I would have been able to do the same in her situation and concluded I could not.

I followed up the Shragai lead a year later, when I was in Florida in 2010, visiting my aunt Petya, the youngest of my Adler aunts and uncles, the last to marry into the clan. I showed her a copy of the Page of Testimony Shragai had filled out for my father's first wife. There was a contact number listed for him, but I had been too timid to call.

Aunt Petya wasn't timid. She dialed the number in Israel and spoke in Hebrew to the person on the other end.

"Was it the man with the fishpond?" I asked when she hung up.

"Ay, Preevaleh," she said with a sigh. "That was Shragai's wife. He died last year, but she said she remembered your father well. Also, she asked about you. She wanted to know if you grew up to be pretty."

"What did you say?"

"What are you talking, what did I say?" my aunt chided me. "I said you were beautiful!"

Sam Kahan and I in 1968 at Shragai's in Kiryat Motzkin

I saw Petya again in 2013 when I took her to lunch and a concert near Boca Raton. While I was driving her home she told me something that nearly sent me skidding off the road.

I had been talking about a young man my father had sent for and taken into his business as an apprentice when I was about twelve. "I wonder whatever happened to him," I mused. "The car-wrecking business was too tough for him, and he went back home to St. Catherine's, Ontario. His name was Jiri Otto."

"A good Czech name," said Aunt Petya. "That was the son of one of your father's girlfriends from Prague, you know."

"My father's *what*?"

"It was long before your mother," Petya said with a laugh. "Why not? Your father was a young man then, very handsome. What your mother hated was that he kept sending parcels and money to this woman, while Chaya wasn't allowed to buy a new winter coat."

I gulped. "Does that mean Jiri is my half-brother?"

Petya gave me a sidelong glance and said nothing. At least it would explain the parcels. My father was normally quite a frugal man.

I thought about the timing. Jiri had come to live near us in Yonkers between 1970 and 1974, when he was in his mid-to-late twenties. My father was in Prague from 1945 to 1947. A child conceived in 1947 or late 1946 would be twenty-five in 1973.

Oh my God, what had Daddy done? And what had my mother thought about all this? It wasn't rocket-science math, after all. Also, it had been weird how Jiri worked alongside my father yet almost never came to our house. He stayed with cousins nearby. My usually warm-hearted mother was cool toward the boy, treating him like hired help.

She must have known.

I called my oldest cousin, Howard, who lived in Portland.

"Right, the *shiksa* from Prague," he said. "Your father loved her very much, but he couldn't marry her because she wasn't Jewish."

I remembered how important it was to my father that a Jewish marriage be aboveboard in all ways. For Howard's wedding, he had used an early speakerphone set-up to assemble a far-flung *beit din*, a rabbinic court, so that Howard's previously married fiancée could be granted a proper Jewish divorce decree.

"But he loved her, right?" I prodded Howard. At least let there be love.

"Oh, yes," he said. "He kept sending her money, right into the 1970s."

I didn't know everything about my father, but I now had a better picture of his romantic timeline: First there was Suri, in Munkach. Then there was the Czech girlfriend, Jiri's mother. Then, there was a short marriage in Israel to Miriam—who, by all accounts, had deceived my father emotionally. He wanted a houseful of children, and she already had two of her own and did not want more. My mother told me, in a lowered voice, that Miriam had terminated a pregnancy without telling my father about it.

Last of all was my mother, who never got the full thirty-three years of marriage she had been promised and who dealt with plenty of challenges during the seventeen years she did get.

But then, as I found out in 2009 after my visit to Yad Vashem, my mother was not an ordinary woman. The Sasa kibbutz where she lived was not an ordinary kibbutz. It was right on the Lebanese border, high up in the mountains near the town of Metulla, the northernmost point in Israel, where it formed part of the band of communal Jewish settlements that helped define the state's borders in 1948. There the soil was thin and the rocks were huge. The group that settled Sasa had nothing but their principles and a few good books, so they had to be strong. The shared privation of those early days brought them closer, which might explain why I received so many responses so quickly when I announced my quest for information through the Shomernet electronic mailing list. People remembered my mother fondly and wanted to help me learn about her.

"We were tall, strong young women who insisted on doing everything the men could do," Rezzie Baum e-mailed back from her home in Tel Aviv. "Your mother and I stacked bales of hay right alongside the guys."

Rezzie wasn't the only one who remembered my mom. Eshel Spiro, who was still at Sasa after fifty years, insisted that I come visit so he could show me something of what my mother's life had been like. Yehuda Beinin, another friend from the listserv, who lived on a nearby kibbutz and whose parents had also known my mother, volunteered to be my guide through the rolling hills of the Galilee. I met Yehuda at his kibbutz, Shomrat, which was on the coast, and we set out, inland and uphill, through mountains that I had last seen in 1968 when they were strewn with barbed wire and warnings of land mines. Now all I saw were luxury vacation villas.

"My mother told me Sasa was poor," I observed. "This area looks very fancy."

"That was a long time ago," Yehuda said.

I love driving on the edge of a car's performance, downshifting to round curves and keeping the tires just on the edge of the pavement so I can send gravel flying. Yehuda's knuckles were white as I drove and he clutched the dashboard.

Finally I saw a sign for Kibbutz Sasa and turned onto a road that ran through apple orchards and past a huge factory that said Plasan Sasa. "They make body armor and armored vehicles here," Yehuda said. "Sasa starved for decades, and now they are the richest kibbutz in Israel."

We parked the car and walked past meadows of blooming cyclamens and poppies. Two dozen schoolchildren dressed as clowns, astronauts, kings, and queens ran by us, laughing. "They're dressed up for Purim," Yehuda said. "They come here from all over."

"But isn't this right on the border? Isn't it dangerous?" I asked.

He shrugged.

An electric cart pulled up and parked in front of the new dining hall. An elderly man climbed out very slowly. "Shalom. Welcome to Sasa," he said. He came closer and looked into my eyes. "Yes, I can see Chaya in you. Come. There's someone who wants to meet you." He guided me inside the dining room and led me to a table of his contemporaries. One of the men stood.

"Do you remember me?" he asked. "It was 1998, and I was wearing this T-shirt." His shirt had a carrot on it and the name of another kibbutz.

I opened my eyes wide. "*Wisconsin*?" I said. "You're the man from the gas station!"

After my mother's death, I inherited the Bubi 2, my mother's 1990 Ford Taurus with the license plate announcing her two grandsons. Originally a neutral black, when the paint got water spots, she had it repainted in a color called ultraviolet, so wherever I drove, people smiled and pointed, especially pimps. In this case, a chance conversation at a gas pump led to the astonishing coincidence that the man in the kibbutz T-shirt I had noticed had actually known my mother back in the day. It was all the more wonderful because my mother had come to me in a dream the night before, with snow-white hair and unbothered by arthritis or other physical ailments. In the dream, I drove her in Bubi 2 to a private airfield, where she boarded an old-fashioned plane from a stairway on the tarmac. Somehow, I knew she was bound for Israel, and I woke with her voice in my head, saying, "Remember, the purpose of life is joy."

Later, when Eshel was showing me the view from his deck, I gazed at the mountains toward Lebanon. They looked familiar. And then I understood.

They looked just like the Santa Cruz Mountains that were visible from Interstate 280 back home. "I don't know what it is, Preeva," my mother used to say. "That view does something to me." It had reminded her of a hopeful time in her life, and now it reminded me of her. That gave me joy.

Eshel Spiro and me on Kibbutz Sasa in 2009

CHAPTER 14

The Guide

My cousin Sam Kahan, twelve years older than I, was like an older brother to me, and he was a good friend, too. I called him Mulku, the name I used when I was a baby, until I was ten. Then his wife, Tirza, insisted I call him Sam, but I didn't mind because she became my friend as well.

Sam was an economist who had worked for a succession of banks, bond houses, and financial institutions, including the Federal Reserve, during his career. He taught, wrote learned papers, and traveled widely to deliver them. This made talking to him very educational. The downside was that when he wasn't being completely silent for hours on end, he spoke at length, which was great in the late 1970s when he was helping me with my college economics papers but not so great when it came to practical, everyday conversation. I knew that when Sam called, I needed to leave half an hour for *hello* and *goodbye*. A simple question about what the weather was like in Chicago would elicit "Consider the following: The usual behavior of the pressure systems around here creates strong winds and freezing rain that the plows can't break through without salt, so the chances are good that Tirza and I will be housebound for a few hours. But it's snowing right now, and the snowplows are doing a pretty good job of pushing the snow aside, so it could be worse."

Sam was my favorite cousin, but I wasn't sure I wanted to travel with him. For years, he had urged me to take a trip with him to Europe to see the town of Munkach, where my father and his mother had grown up as siblings, but Tirza's stories of her husband's sense of direction—and my observation that he missed my son's bar mitzvah because he went forty miles in the wrong direction, gave me pause. Tirza said that Sam was a quirky traveler who loved striking out on his own, taking impossibly long walks in utter silence, and getting completely lost.

Also, Sam Kahan followed many rules but I did not. He had been raised strictly Orthodox, with a *yeshiva* education and a set of strictures on what he could eat and when he could travel. All he could have in nonkosher restaurants was tuna fish and raw vegetables, and every time he sat down to a meal he paused and his lips moved, which I knew meant he was praying. He put absolutely no pressure on me to join him in these observances, but like many liberal Jews, they reminded me of all I was not doing to support my Jewishness.

After I confessed that I couldn't identify all the people in my father's photos and told Sam how I had not gotten to see the family tree that had hung on Ludwig's wall, he renewed his campaign to get me to Eastern Europe to see the town we still referred to as Munkach. (In 1945 it became Mukachevo, part of the USSR, but with the breakup of the Soviet Union the town became part of Ukraine and received the more Ukrainian spelling of Mukacheve.)

While under Soviet control, the town was practically unreachable, but later, as part of Ukraine, it was easier to visit. By then you didn't even need a visa. "Let's go, just you and me," Sam said. I stared at him through the phone. "It'll be fun," he insisted.

"Fun?" I finally answered. "We're talking about Ukraine, Sam." I had visited Yalta and Odessa on a cruise ten years before.

"When I was there in 1999 it was nothing but decay covered in scaffolding. It's not for tourists," I said.

"The economy is better now," he insisted.

"So, maybe less scaffolding, but how will we get to Munkach? It's way out in the middle of nowhere."

"We'll rent a car."

"How will we know where we're going?"

"We'll read signs and maps."

"Do you read Russian or Ukrainian?"

"No, but I speak lots of other languages," he said. "We'll manage somehow."

I didn't want to manage somehow in the country that invented pogroms.

"We're getting a guide," I said.

"Won't that be pricey?"

"It's cheaper than being kidnapped and held for ransom."

He agreed, and we went on what is now called a roots trip to Ukraine, at the end of June in 2010. I hired Alex Dunai, the guide who had helped the author Daniel Mendelsohn when he was researching his bestselling memoir *The Lost*. Alex Dunai is a historian who has devoted his life to helping Jews explore their ancestors' lives in Galicia. He is extremely famous in genealogical circles and is so much in demand that, to reach him, you have to go through a third party.

In the book, Alex is described as an affable bear of a man. He has devoted his life to helping Jews find connections to their history and was a judo champion to boot. This makes him an ideal guide. But our first meeting must have given him a less than ideal impression of me. The first time I saw him in person was at the terminal of the L'viv airport. I was a bit discombobulated. The immigration and customs entry procedure for Ukraine had been chaotic—the customs lounge looked like a post office, and I had filled out forms without really understanding the instructions and handed them to officials that looked about fifteen and who could neither read nor speak much English. Customs officials who spoke even less English had just searched my luggage, and my carefully packed suitcase had been messed up by the procedure.

"Is that your underwear?" asked a man who was about six feet tall and four feet wide, with black hair and a chin like Kirk Douglas. He pointed to the floor behind me where two pairs of my panties had not quite made it back during the repack.

"Yes," I said. "Are you Alex?"

We shook hands, and I gathered up my panties. As I tried to stuff them back into my suitcase, the latches popped, and the case burst open. My new guide held my purse as I repacked my wardrobe. Then we sat down and waited for Sam, who arrived without any of his underwear hanging out.

Alex took us around in a Mitsubishi sport-utility vehicle he had just bought. He pointed out the university where he studied history fifteen years ago, the roads that led to different Ukrainian towns, and the central plaza of L'viv, where the oldest buildings were and which included the Jewish section. The old town of L'viv escaped bombing in the war and has a great deal of charm. He showed us the old Jewish section, where a "Jewish" restaurant serves nonkosher food. He even showed us, with particular relish, a bronze statue of Leopold von Sacher-Masoch, the writer and journalist from whose name is derived the term masochism. Although not a Jew, von Sacher-Masoch is L'viv's most famous contributor to modern culture.

We spent our first night in a hotel in L'viv and got on the road early the next morning. We drove to Nadvirna, a town with an actual kosher restaurant where we ate lunch. Nadvirna is in the district of Ivano-Frankivsk but sits near the edge of Transcarpathia, historically known as Carpathian Ruthenia, a huge area used mostly for agriculture and vacations. As soon as we crossed into Transcarpathia, the mountains began. As we headed uphill, the road became a disaster. It consisted of two narrow lanes, one in each direction, with frequent potholes between stretches that were patched. Gravel and degraded asphalt rattled against the bottom of the vehicle. The sides of the road weren't marked with yellow stripes and reflectors, as in California, but with narrow dirt shoulders, some leading into gullies, some into brush. We shared the road with logging trucks filled with second-growth trees. It was terrifying. I would have preferred to be the one at the wheel; at least I'd have only myself to blame for the inevitable crash.

Alex knew how to navigate those roads, and there was no crash, except for the punk rock on the car stereo. To my surprise, Alex listened to the same defiant bands, like the Clash and the Sex Pistols, I had listened to in college, and I sang along with Sid Vicious and UB40, since I knew most of the lyrics. Alex was puzzled by my cousin and me and kept asking questions he didn't think we could answer. My cousin had spent his life in travel and pious study and I had spent decades gardening and traveling, so our fields of knowledge were very different from each other and wide enough that we had the questions covered. When Alex asked us why the horses we passed had red tassels hanging from their harnesses, Sam immediately said, "Superstition. To keep away the evil eye."

Alex pointed out a strange globular green growth in an oak. "What do you think *that* might be?" he asked, ready for his big triumph.

"What, you mean the mistletoe?" I said. He looked deflated.

Alex was quick as a snake. That was the only way he could have driven as smoothly as he did, steering around the potholes as large as Fiats and doing it so well we hit very few. He had to have a Diet Coke in his hand every second. Every two hours, we stopped at a filling station to buy another. Alex also had a peculiar habit of closing his eyes at the wheel; perhaps he suffered from sleep apnea. After the third stop in four hours, I had an idea.

"How about we keep a cooler of Diet Cokes in the car?" I suggested.

"Why should we do that?" Alex asked suspiciously. He liked his separation of car and store, I guess.

"So we can drive more than two hours at a time. These constant stops are getting on my nerves," I said.

It took me a day and a half to convince him that keeping a cooler of Diet Cokes in the car would make our trip go faster. We didn't even look to set one up until we got to Munkach; then it took nearly as long to find such a thing. At one covered market, I could have bought cheap shoes or engine parts or tacky garlands of tinsel and fake flowers to put on graves, but no cooler—and no Diet Coke.

Finally, at a supermarket, we found the diet soda but no coolers. This supermarket was *the* huge modern place to buy food in town, probably more expensive than the smaller more rustic markets, but I didn't care. It had bulk frozen vegetable bins where you scooped out as much as you wanted. It had more forms of dairy products than I had ever seen before. There was an entire stand-alone cooler full of different kinds of caviar. The liquor section had ten rows, three of which were devoted to vodka. One row had vodka in unusually shaped bottles, including lady's slippers, castles, and penises. We just got the Diet Coke and got out of there. We eventually found a soft-sided, insulated cooler at an auto parts store.

I had an unhealthy fixation on keeping to our carefully planned itinerary. Sam and I had spent months negotiating that itinerary with Alex and each other via e-mail during the winter. The three of us could have negotiated peace in the Middle East faster. One of the problems was that Sam and I were both looking for our fathers, but mine had grown up in Munkach, his father had grown up in Szurte, and Sam's father's relatives had lived in various Hungarian towns. It was Sam's mother who was our blood connection. I could hardly blame him for being more interested in the Kahan side, but Sam's idea of researching family was to visit as many graveyards as possible. This made no sense to me, and I had said as much when we were discussing the trip on the phone.

"But Sam, you're a Kohen; you can't go into graveyards," I argued. As a member of the ancient Jewish priestly tribe, the ones that deliver a special blessing to the people on Yom Kippur and traditionally have the honor of reading Torah first, he observed the religious law that forbids contact with dead bodies. When my father was buried, Sam had waited by the cemetery gate and said Kaddish out on the sidewalk. Perhaps that was the reason for his fascination with graveyards; they were technically forbidden to him.

"It'll be fine," Sam had said. "You'll read me the gravestones over the fence."

"My Hebrew's not that good."

"Then you'll take pictures and show me."

The way this worked out in practice was that I took pictures, but the pictures were too small for Sam to read on camera, so I'd upload the photos in the evening to my computer, and he would pause over each one for an outrageous amount of time until I poked him.

"Sam!"

"What?"

"Could any of these be our relatives?"

"Well they *could* be, on some level."

"Do they match the names we have?"

"No."

"So, what level are you talking about? Move on to the next page! Come on, we're only here for three days!"

The first official stop on our quest for our ancestors was Verkhine Vodiane, also called Velkhiy Blchiv, which we thought our ancestors called Vysni Apsa. It is not far from the town of Rachiv, and it is where Sam and I thought our grandfather Chaim David Adler had been born. The land-owning records of the Kingdom of Hungary assembled for taxation in the year 1828 have at least five Adlers in the town. There was a Jewish school and a synagogue, long since converted to other uses, but there was no Jewish cemetery in evidence. But where there are Jews, there are cemeteries, so we veered off the main road and followed a dirt road up a hill in the direction a villager had pointed us. Then we separated and went in different directions to look for the graveyard of the Jews. Sam went downhill. Alex patrolled the middle territory. I went uphill, tramping over the lush grass among the flowers scattered on the hillside. The herbs in the grass beneath my feet released a sweet perfume. The clouds lifted for a few moments and I could see the surrounding hills. Finally, I could breathe. It was the first time I was alone on this trip, but it was a short-lived respite. I had to reconnect with Alex and Sam and announce I had not found any cemeteries, but then, neither had they.

The three of us were about to leave when Alex noticed the heel of a woman's dress shoe lying by a dirt track. "Maybe there's something around here," he said. His instincts were right on. I threaded my way through the trees and found a clearing full of scattered stones and a few graves with restored headstones. I took photos. I caught a glimpse of grey in the thicker trees beyond, on a hillside, where I found more headstones, fallen and half buried. There were the remains of some old oil lamps on sticks in the ground nearby. Ukrainians spend a lot of time and money on their graves, adorning them with huge wreaths and visiting them for family picnics on Sundays after church. They sometimes wonder how the Jews have let the graves of their ancestors get into such sorry states. I took more pictures, and Sam looked at them, but in the end, the graves did not seem to hold any Adlers.

Next, Sam wanted to see Szurte, his father's hometown. Szurte is a small place ten miles from Munkach. The drive there took two hours. At a modern gas station on the outskirts of Szurte, Sam spoke to an attendant in Hungarian. The man gestured toward the fields behind the station. "He says there's a Jewish graveyard back there!" Sam said.

We tramped back there, about one hundred yards from the road in a field. The pasture there was fairly level, and the grass and weeds had been kept in check by grazing animals. Once we got to the graveyard, though, there was an eight-foot cement wall surrounding it, with a sign proudly proclaiming that the wall was courtesy of a group called Avoysenu, based in Brooklyn. I wanted to march straight over to Brooklyn and give this group a piece of my mind. The wall had served to keep the animals out and, therefore, the weeds high. "We would all be better off if they had not built this wall," I said to no one in particular, "The grazing animals would have kept the weeds down and we could have seen the headstones." All I could see through the gate were nettles, stinging nettles, the jellyfish of the plant kingdom. When I tried to push them aside, I got stung, a high-voltage pain like electricity that prickled my skin like fifty wasp stings at once. "What do you see? What do you see?" shouted Sam, standing far off in safety. "I see the need for a gas-powered weed whacker," I shouted. I limped back to the gas station with red patches on my arms and no insight into the walled-off site's inhabitants. At least we found a living link to Sam's history. In Szurte, we located the house where Sam's father's family had lived and took pictures of it. Then it was time to see my father's hometown of Munkach.

CHAPTER 15

The Locked Gate

It took twenty minutes to drive from Szurte to Munkach. The two places were very different. Szurte was a small town; Munkach was a metropolis. It had several main streets and a cobbled town square, which anchored a main street that had a planted median with bronze statues every fifty yards. The town hall looked like it had been built in the eighteenth century and had a fresh coat of apple-green paint. A wide, shallow river divided the town, which spread out on both sides of the water. The style of the homes was different as well. Whereas the homes in Szurte were separated by wide side yards and set back from the street, the homes in Munkach were very close together, separated by alleys, with the buildings right on the sidewalk. I had seen this style of building in Yalta, Odessa, and Lódź; there were probably large courtyards behind the buildings, I reasoned. We checked into the Star Hotel, which was actually owned by a man in Brooklyn named Roth. The lobby had beautiful dark woodwork framing an impressive fireplace, although it would have looked better by the light of something other than what was there, a few fluorescent bulbs that gave the place a bluish tinge.

The bellman ushered us upstairs to our rooms, and with great solemnity showed me some sort of paper-wrapped lozenge that went into a round, vented gizmo the size of a ping-pong ball that plugged into the wall.

"Alex, what is this guy showing me?" I asked.

"How to refresh your insecticide dispenser."

Eeeew, I thought.

After stowing our luggage, we walked over to the Great Synagogue of Munkach, now under scaffolding, and then rounded the corner to the Jewish center, a cluster of three buildings that included an old synagogue, a single-story dining room and administration building, and a multistory dorm for the masses of Hasidim that swept through to visit the grave of the Munkacher rebbe from time to time. The old synagogue reminded me of the dusty wooden sanctuary where my father had taken me in the Bronx. In the administration building we found Bumi Leibovitch—who, as Alex proudly announced, was head of the Munkach Jewish community, comprised mostly of Russians who had retired there. Alex had assembled a list of six addresses from the documents Sam and I provided—three where our parents and grandparents had lived and three where my father had lived with his first wife, Suri—and Bumi was going to explain how the street names had changed and what the streets were now called. I had been hoping to see a huge, old parchment with copperplate writing and was disappointed to see him pull out the same map anyone could have downloaded from JewishGen.

As Alex and Bumi conferred, I thought about what I wanted to find. Now that I was physically in the very town where my father grew up, I hoped to run into all sorts of people who remembered him or members of his family. I started with Bumi. "Did you know any Adlers from"—I let Alex finish the sentence because I could not pronounce the name of the town that we knew as Vysni Apsa.

"Yes," he said, and I was overjoyed. His wife's father had been an Adler from that village. But this Adler had never married his wife's mother and in any case had died in the late 1940s—a dead end.

Sam and I decided to visit the addresses in chronological order, the oldest document first. We started with our grandparents' wedding record, house number twenty-four on Latoryzcna, "the Jewish street." It was a one-story stucco with many chimneys. "This is probably how it looked in 1908," said Alex, who had an eye for period architecture.

A bank on the corner of the Jewish street and the main street had a pictorial plaque of the gates to the Jewish ghetto of Munkach and an inscription dedicated to the town's Jews. The houses on the Jewish street had backyards that bordered a park overlooking the river. Across from the Jewish street, in the other direction, opposite the river, was a huge vacant lot covered in rubble; that's where the rest of the Jewish section had been.

The second address, listed on my uncle Mendy's birth certificate, was where our grandparents and their children—five at the time, including Sam's mother and my father, two older girls, and my uncle Mendy—had lived for a short time. The green-painted building had received several architectural add-ons over the years, according to Alex, and was now located smack in the middle of the town's commercial center.

The third address we had for our parents was 48 Havlickova, a few streets over from the busy center of town and across from a municipal building that looked like a police station. This was where my father spent most of his childhood, from 1919 to 1939. The house had recently been divided into multiple residences. "Look, my mom's pear tree!" said Sam when we walked around the perimeter to the big backyard.

"Silly, it's not the same tree," I said. Probably every yard in Munkach had a fruit tree, and I doubted that any of them lived ninety years.

At each address, as we took copious pictures, I gradually felt a dizziness settle over me. It wasn't because I was walking on the same streets as my father once did; it was because the addresses we had saved for the afternoon were the ones where he had lived with a wife who wasn't my mother and with a daughter who wasn't me.

The three of us fortified ourselves with pizza (well, hand-thrown crust with tomato sauce and melted cheese) before continuing. We sat in a café opposite the town taxi stand, exactly where my father probably started his taxi-driving career.

I was still feeling woozy but couldn't put it off any longer—it was time to find the three addresses where my father had lived with his first wife, Sarolta Kahan, Suri, mother of the girl on the wall, my shadow sister.

The first address, from their 1939 marriage certificate, when Samuel Armin Adler was twenty-eight and newly married: 24 Lord Rothmere. It was a five-story apartment building that had been built in the 1920s or '30s in the Bauhaus style, close to the main synagogue, on a park by the banks of the river that runs through Munkach. We could tell by the ten mailboxes that it had two apartments per floor and by looking at the outside that each apartment had its own outdoor space in the form of two terraces apiece. There was a small garden out back by the main entrance. (Most residential buildings in Munkach have their front doors in the backyard along a common courtyard.) I walked through the garden, noting that it had been tended at one time but needed a good weeding and greeting a cat that came up to rub against my leg, and marveled at how much the building reminded me of similar buildings in Tel Aviv and Haifa, where people settled in apartments for their whole lives, not as a stopgap dwelling before moving to suburbia and buying a house.

How my mother would have loved to start her married life in such a place with my father—a new building with two terraces near the river, instead of the tenement at 50 Hunts Point Avenue where they lived when they were first married.

"Don't you want to knock on the door and see inside?" Alex prodded me.

"That's okay. I'll take pictures," I mumbled. I was already shutting down emotionally, the way I do when life gets too complicated.

The second address, 50 Korosveg, was from the 1940 birth certificate of the first child, the boy, Bela. This was a one-story house closer to the center of town, on a busy street near a hospital and restaurants. We went down the alley to the door in the rear and found that the building had been divided— "probably before 1940," as per Alex—into four apartments. There was a large yard with clotheslines and fruit trees and a huge hydrangea. Two outbuild-ings that had been garages or used for storage had been converted into living spaces, "probably after the war," Alex observed.

A few houses further down the same street was the third address, 58 Korosveg. This was from 1941, and it was from the birth certificate that indicated where Hajmalka, the girl on the wall, had lived. It was the house that I wanted to see most and least. It was perfectly fitting, then, that it was the only house that proved inaccessible to us—the path that should have led to the backyard was covered with a metal gate and a padlock. "This means it only belongs to one family," Alex said. "If there were a shared driveway, they wouldn't be able to lock it like this."

The building was about the same size as the one that had been turned into four units, which meant quite a lot of space for one family. Suri had lived in her own big house, and my father had had his own private driveway. It must have spoiled him. When my parents were shopping for a possible house in Yonkers, he wouldn't even consider a shared driveway. "Preeva, I'm sorry," my mother used to say when I complained that my father had reneged on his promise to buy a house for us to live in so I could have a puppy. "Your father lived the best years of his life already, and we only have what's left."

But standing in the street in front of my father's old house, I couldn't be angry with him, so I deflected it into an irrational rage at Suri. She had gotten everything my mother had wanted. It was hard for me in that moment to recall how short-lived Suri's glory had been. She did have a house of her own—but not for very long. The address on Hajmalka's birth certificate was from 1941. In 1943 Suri would have to take her young chil-dren and hide in the woods. Later, all three of them would be rounded up and all three would die in the concentration camps.

The photos that plagued me, complete with their gold frames, had been hanging on the wall at 54 Korosveg. My father got them back after the war simply by knocking on the door and asking for them from the house's current occupants. He also appeared before a judge and filed a "declaration of damages" with the Munkach town council—essentially a receipt for what was lost during the war—in addition to taking other measures to try to reclaim his property. He took his pictures and his receipt and moved to Prague, never to return. "What would I do, cry over the ground?" he used to say.

And yet, here I was, his one remaining child, locked outside his old gate, wondering how and why he had prospered enough during the war years to have a private house that size. From the fashionable apartment in 1939, to the multifamily house in 1940, to the private home in 1942—in three short years, my father and Suri had moved up so quickly. How had he afforded it? In the years from 1938 to 1944, Munkach was under the rule of the Hungarians, who were under Hitler. How had my father managed it? He had proudly admitted that he passed for German on trains, but did that mean he was not the war hero I had always thought him to be—that I wanted him to be?

I thought about his story about trading tires for coffee. When he was fixing German trucks in the forced labor brigade, he was allowed to put on his *t'fillin* once a day and *daven*, "pray."

And then it hit me: My father's wheeling, dealing, and horse-trading had provided a better standard of living for this family than my mother and I had had. Here, in this small backwater town, they had respected him enough to leave his wedding portraits and paintings on the wall of the house he lived in with a family that disappeared with the wave of a baton at Auschwitz. How had he achieved this success? Had he been a smuggler?

"Alex, I need to go to city hall and look up a few things," I said, feeling faint.

"It's closed today. What would you like to know?"

"Did my father actually own this house? Maybe he just rented it." Please, I thought, let my father have been too poor to own a house. Let my mother at least have that in common with Suri.

"Even if city hall were open now, there's no way you would find owner-ship records from that period," Alex said. "Those records were destroyed by the Germans."

"Okay, then, where did the Judenrat meet when Munkach was occu-pied?" This question was related to another of my father's stories, which I told Alex. "My father said he had supplies of explosives ready to blow up the Munkach railroad tunnel, but he got called into the offices of the Judenrat and told not to use them. I want to see the room where it happened." I had imagined the scene many times, in that room where he changed his mind. Later he would say that the greatest regret of his life was not blowing up the tunnel.

"You want to find an office used by the Jews during an occupation that was over sixty years ago?" said Alex.

"Some of the people here look old enough to remember those times. Could you ask them?"

"Preeva, these people don't know anything about that time. They came here after the war to work at the Soviet air force base or to retire. This kind of detail is impossible to find now. What else do you want?"

"I want the kind of experience where the family invites you in for coffee and brings down a chest of treasures from the attic," I said.

"Maybe something like that happens on the second or third visit to a place, but you are only here for two days." Alex said. "Look, you saw where your parents grew up. You walked around their yards, took pictures. You're lucky. You found every address on your list. You saw all the places where your father and his first wife lived. All those houses are still standing. That's more than most people get to see. Isn't that enough? You should be more excited."

I wasn't excited. I was exhausted. We dined that night with the Jews of Munkach—the men and women at separate tables, as per Orthodox custom. I sat with a bunch of older women who only spoke Yiddish and Russian. I spent the evening nodding and smiling, not understanding a single word.

It was raining the next morning. I stayed in bed as long as I could. I had no desire to do anything. I could not find the Judenrat or speak the language or find anything to confirm or deny my growing suspicion that my father had prospered unduly under the Germans.

I just wanted to go home.

PART III

Everything Is a Miracle

CHAPTER 16

Memory of the Planet

Shortly after I returned from Mukacheve, I started searching the Internet for traces of my father and his family. Almost all the sources I searched were Jewish: JewishGen, *The Encyclopedia of Jewish Life Before and During the Holocaust*, *Encyclopedia Judaica*. It got me thinking: who, exactly, is a Jew?

This question will no doubt be debated until the end of time, with as many definitions as there are Jews. In my temple, Congregation Etz Chayim in Palo Alto, we rewrote our bylaws to define a Jew as anyone who self-identifies as one.

But how do we know? How do we keep track?

When a group takes a bus for an outing, many of them use a buddy system to make sure they don't lose anyone at a rest stop or concession stand. "Hey, everyone, look around to see who's missing!" the driver calls out, and you make sure your mom is aboard, or Timmy. Once everyone's buddy is present, the bus can move along again.

The buddy system is not foolproof. My friends Jeanne and Beth were once abandoned at a restaurant in Massachusetts. Still, it mostly works. Maybe that's why my cousin Tirza always recommends joining organizations when you move to a new neighborhood. "It's a great way to settle into a place," she says. "You join an organization, and then if, God forbid, you get hit by a car, someone notices you're gone."

The way Jews keep track of each other is by showing up at celebrations of Passover, Rosh Hashanah, and Yom Kippur—all the holidays that Jewish mothers guilt their children into attending. It's our way of keeping track of who is on our bus. These gatherings are important because Jews have a history of wandering, and we don't want to leave anyone behind.

There is another way to keep track of who is on the bus: genealogical research. You look up old documents and photos and put them together with what you hear from your oldest family members and re-create a picture of lost times. It was Rabbi Shmuley Boteach who brought the importance of that home to me.

I was in Washington, DC, to hear him speak before a genealogy conference. Rabbi Shmuley had three claims to fame: he had written a bestseller, *Kosher Sex*; he was host of his own cable-television reality show, *Shalom in the Home*, where he went into people's houses and used Jewish values to make peace—shalom—among warring family members; and, most important to me, he had debated religion and God with Christopher Hitchens, the brilliant English writer and marquee atheist who later died in 2011. Boteach didn't win the debate—few could win against Hitchens—but it took guts to try at all. I admired that, particularly because my husband's atheism made my life miserable. "Have a nice delusion," he would say when I left the house for Saturday morning services, referring to fellow atheist Richard Dawkins's book *The God Delusion*. "How was the fairy-tale book club?" he would say when I came home. I got back at him by telling people, "My husband goes to meetings where people jump to their feet, wave their hands in the air, and holler, 'Hallelujah! We don't believe!'"

Rabbi Shmuley was an add-on to the first genealogy conference I attended, in Washington, DC, in 2011. I went to declare my allegiance with the Jewish dogma. Unfortunately, I arrived too late to catch the rabbi's remarks. I showed up for the after-dinner speech and found dinner over and what I had imagined as a large banquet to be a small room with maybe fifty places with nothing on the tables but crumbs of challah, stale pats of margarine, and empty water glasses. People were singing the after-dinner blessing, and the rabbi's talk had taken place an hour before.

I was furious. The conference program had specifically said that the speech was after dinner—why had it happened early? It brought up all sorts of issues for me—about feeling like an outsider, about reconciliation between Jews who drive on Shabbat and those who don't (I had driven there on a Saturday), about orthodoxy versus liberalism and about being an only child in a world of multiple siblings.

I went right up to the rabbi's table and stated my complaint. To my surprise, he apologized. "I'm very sorry for the misunderstanding," he said.

I asked him if he could please summarize the talk I had missed, and he did. "I spoke about internal identity versus external identity," he said. "External identity is what we do, our titles, what we have. Internal identity is who we are. Genealogy is important because it is taking your ancestors, who are anonymous, and honoring them because they are important to who you are. Celebrity worship is very common in this country, and it involves idolizing people who are famous but who have nothing to do with you. But when you take anonymous people who are important to you, and recognize them, that is about discovering who you are." Discovering who I was—in addition to being another girl on the communal bus of Jews or a pale substitute for the girl on the wall, my shadow sister, had become more important to me after my fiftieth birthday. That was when the gaps in my knowledge had been exposed by that conversation with Leonard's cousin Lottie after my slide show and my ignorance about the identity of my father's second wife. "You have such an interesting background," Lottie had said. "I had no idea."

The enterprise of discovering who we—the human race—are has been taken up by the Mormons, who are determined to trace the lineage of every human being back to Adam and Eve. They store their records in bunkers in the mountains above Salt Lake City. Mormons are obsessed with who is related to whom by blood or marriage because, according to their criteria, they can claim dead people as kin, baptize them posthumously (even if the dead had a different religion when alive), inscribe them in a record book, and expect to keep company with them in heaven. Some Mormons actually claim to have traced their ancestry back to Adam and Eve. And to be close to their ancestors in perpetuity, Mormons claim them formally by baptizing them. They've decided they don't need an actual physical body (or permission) to baptize, that documentary evidence of a person's existence and connection to an existing member of the faith is enough.

Converting the heathen to Mormonism is one of their key missions, and to that end they sent missionaries around the world, particularly to Europe after World War I, to photograph and microfilm every birth and death record they could find, in every city hall, church, and hamlet. Mormons posthumously converted Holocaust victims until the outcry from the Jewish community made them stop in 2009. Twenty years ago, to help with creating family histories, the Church of Jesus Christ of Latter-Day Saints began putting its records online at Family Search (www.family search.org). Before that, you had to go to a Family History Center—there are more than 4,700 scattered around the world—where, for a fee, you could have a roll of microfilm sent so you could copy the entries for your ancestors to add to your own family tree.

There's a Family History Center in Oakland, California, where I attended a lecture on how to search for Hungarian Jews in Europe. It was in the basement of one of the low buildings clustered around the Oakland Temple, a tall abstract structure that looks like a cross between a Soviet ministry building and Buck Rogers's rocket ship, situated on ten acres of tidy lawns, pretty flowers, sculpted shrubs, 1960s fountains, and parking lots. Inside was a library devoted to genealogy, with microfiche readers and books on genealogy and world history. There was a rack of pamphlets with translations of common genealogical terms in various languages. I took the pamphlets for Czech and Hungarian.

Mormonism has only been around for about two hundred years. Before the Mormons were fascinated by genealogy, local historians were fascinated by blood connections of prominent families—just ask the Daughters of the American Revolution. The Brits have their Burke's Peerage, a publication and organization founded in 1826 to keep track of British royalty and that has established a style of narrative genealogy. The Maoris in New Zealand sing their children to sleep with a litany of their ancestors. There used to be, and still may be, parents who check the lineage of their children's friends to avoid play dates with a "non"—non-Jew, non-Catholic, non–Mayflower descendent, whatever.

The Mormons aren't the only game in town. Different information can be found in period maps, newspapers, and business directories. For example, I found my grandfather's name in a digital copy of business directories from Galicia, an area that often changed hands between Poland and Russia. The Radix database, run by library researcher Janos Bogardi at Janus-Pannonius University in Pecs, Hungary, has records for the Austro-Hungarian Empire dating back three hundred years.

Records are going on the Internet at greater and greater speed, powered by personal computers and people's desire to trace their roots. Companies like Ancestry.com, Archives.com, MyHeritage.com, and Geni .com make a big business of being web portals to the past. For $50.00 a year, Ancestry.com lets you see US records on your home computer, and for another $250.00 you can also view records from all over the world. I bought the international access. Archives.com costs $39.95 a year, and I bought a subscription to that site, also. Many libraries have access to these databases, and you can see what is in them for free, but you have to leave home. Personally, I keep track of the genealogical databases through *Nu? What's New?* a weekly e-zine from the publishers of *Avotaynu*, a quarterly subscription-based journal of Jewish genealogy run by Gary Mokotoff, whose first career was in computer science.

Early in my search, I joined JewishGen, a web portal that is the repository of the efforts of thousands of volunteers who do their own research and share their findings online with each other and the world. They post reports of their journeys back to ancestral homes, read tombstones, decipher and transcribe Jewish documents, and type their findings into Excel spreadsheets and databases to upload to JewishGen. This huge undertaking is done mostly by ordinary people who want to honor their ancestors and pay forward the help they received from other "genners" during their own quests.

The Internet can provide virtual towns for real memories. All over cyberspace, people and institutions are building pages and constructing databases to memorialize lost people and places. There are web pages that record family trips to old shtetls, created by family members who go. Yad Vashem has a good directory of towns where Jews used to live, along with pronunciation guides and historical footage and maps. JewishGen has a host of pages called KehilaLinks, with more towns than Yad Vashem has, recording every place where ten Jews ever got together. Entire museums exist online, and many families use them as a starting point for research and planning. It's a way to keep information safe and take up even less space than microfilm and microfiche. JewishGen, is now "powered by Ancestry.com," which means that the Ancestry.com servers hold the JewishGen data, so that now, just as you're making a bit of real progress as you dig down from one JewishGen web page to the next, Ancestry.com kicks in and asks for your credit card. But is it safe? What if, God forbid, the Nazis rise again? Will they find us online? The Internet has shrunk the world, but that only amplified my paranoia.

I wanted to learn more about my father and what he had done in his youth and also about his family. Unfortunately, as my fascination with the past grew, so did a raging case of technophobia, which only made my pursuit of facts about my father harder. Computers are all about shortcuts, but you can't get where you're going if you don't pay the proper attention.

My early plunge into online genealogy in 2008 was a failure because I kept getting lost. That was another reason to go the 2011 conference of the International Association of Jewish Genealogical Societies, an umbrella group of seventy-four Jewish genealogical societies worldwide. Their conference was being held in Washington, DC, and included a track of classes for beginners. Through them, I hoped to see the path ahead for finding out about ancestors as more resources became available online.

My raging technophobia amused my children and infuriated my husband, who didn't understand it. I, myself, didn't understand how I had lost my grip on using personal computers. I studied programming in high school and college back in the days of PL/I (Programming Language One) and COBOL (Common Business Oriented Language). I learned on punch cards and graduated to Gandalf terminals in college, then worked on Univacs in Murray Hill, New Jersey. My husband had helped design two of the first personal computers, the Commodore PET and its successor, the VIC-20. After we married, he helped design the Atari ST. Because he had been in charge of process engineering for a year at Commodore on the LCD (liquid-crystal display) chip line and grasped the physics, he understood computing and computers on a molecular level.

He did his best to explain it to me. I asked him to open up an old VIC-20 and interpret what I saw:

"What's the green stuff with holes?" I asked him.

"It's called breadboard."

"And the shiny paths?"

"Circuits."

"So what are those spidery things, again?"

"Chips."

"And the little candy canes and lentils?"

"Resistors and capacitors."

I knew just enough to be dangerous, crashing every computer Len brought home from work and then calling him at the office for free customer support. "The memory in the computer. It says it's running out!" I called in a panic.

"What memory?"

"The *computer* memory!"

"What did you do to it, Peebs?" he asked, annoyed that I was breaking the spell he was under when he programmed.

"I don't know. I was pressing some buttons and it went blank."

"You must have been doing something wrong," he insisted. "Things don't go wrong for no reason. I programmed that machine. Computers don't do anything on their own without input. Did you try pressing the escape key?"

"If you loved me you would just fix it," I told him, quite reasonably.

Len knew memory. He revered it. One of his prized possessions was a piece of "core" from one of the first computers ever made. It was green and rectangular and must have weighed five pounds. It looked like shiny window screening. I took the "core" to an art store and had it framed to keep the dust off.

For a while, when Len was at Atari, he gave me beta versions of software that he thought was running smoothly because he knew I would probably break it in five seconds. That way he could troubleshoot a product before it went to market.

I would call him at work, minutes after he arrived at his office. "Honey, it's busted," I would say of the latest beta gizmo.

"It's okay," Len said. "You're just helping me do my job. In my business, we make something idiot proof; then they make a better idiot."

I was one of the best.

While researching my trip to Ukraine, my forays into the records of JewishGen went later and later into the night as I sought to find people who knew Adlers in Carpathian Ruthenia. I did find them in the uncle of Randy Schoenberg, the head of the Austria-Czech Special Interest Group on JewishGen. He put me in touch with his uncle. His uncle spoke to me in 2010, after I came back from the trip to the Ukraine, still smarting from my failure to find anyone who knew the Adlers when I was in Munkach.

"Yes, I knew the Adlers" he said. "They ran the taxi service."

"Didn't they also sell cars?"

"Maybe on the side, from time to time. I remember hanging around their taxi stand when I was a little boy. Mostly they drove people from Munkach to Ungvar."

This connection cemented my loyalty to JewishGen forever.

Another source of information on the towns and Jews before the war is Spielberg's Visual History Archive. Shortly after the movie *Schindler's List* was released in 1993, director Steven Spielberg funded an oral-history drive to get as many Holocaust survivors on videotape as possible. Today there are nearly 52,000 interviews in the Visual History Archives, housed and indexed at the University of Southern California (although you can access them at one of forty-eight sites worldwide). The experience of telling their stories proved so beneficial to the genocide survivors that a group called the Shoah Foundation, also based at USC, expanded the practice. The Shoah archive also now collects video interviews of survivors of genocides in Rwanda, Cambodia, and Armenia.

Before my trip with my cousin Sam to Ukraine, I accessed the archives to see if I could find out anything else about my father. That attempt mostly failed because I couldn't listen to any of the oral-history tapes for long without collapsing into a blubbering mass of tears and regret upon hearing the Munkach accent. I did manage to find one Morris Baron, an old man from Florida who claimed that an Adler had given him a ride to Munkach right after the war. When I called him, he described the Adler who gave him a ride, and it was one of my father's brothers, Willy, my aunt Petya's husband. Willy died fifteen years after my father. I called Petya to let her know what I had found, and she was not surprised. "Willy saved many people this way, including a little girl whose entire family was drowned in the Dnieper," she said. "Willy hid her under a seat in the truck he was driving and got her to safety. So many years later, she came to visit us in Yonkers, to say thank you."

"What did he tell her?" I asked my aunt.

"Willy said, 'You're welcome.' What else would we tell her?"

So Morris Baron was just another survivor in Florida who had been helped by Willy. I got my aunt's consent to give him her number so he could thank her personally. He called and asked the widow of the man who saved him for a date.

CHAPTER 17

First Cousin, Three Times Removed

Somewhere in the basement of a synagogue in Brooklyn, my mother insisted, was a family tree with my name on it. My cousin Sam Kahan had seen a copy of this tree in Israel, in my late uncle Ludwig's apartment. This tree—a framed document—was among the items of my uncle's that I hoped to see on my journeys to Israel in 2009, 2011, and 2012. Unfortunately, Ludwig's children couldn't bear to go through their father's old belongings to search for it.

The purpose of the family tree, according to my mother, was to remind everyone on it that they had family connections, or *yichus*. She would mutter under her breath, "*Yichus, tuchus*," which roughly translates to "merit through family connections, my ass." My mother had quickly tired of the discussions of *yichus* that went on when she visited my father's cousins. The cousins were Hasidim who assiduously kept track of how close they were to the great scholar in their family, the first Spinka Rebbe Yosef Meir Weiss. All of them enjoyed the benefit of his merit through their family ties, but my mother did not, since *yichus* apparently only travels through blood. Rebbe Yosef Meir Weiss was a scholar of some note who lived from 1838 to 1909 and wrote the *Imrei Yosef*, a book by which he is sometimes called. He has his own entry in the *Encyclopedia Judaica*. The followers of this rebbe were ultraobservant. Pruve Weiss—my grandmother and my namesake—was the connection to these cousins. She was a grandniece of the Spinka Rebbe on her father's side. She believed in strict observance of Jewish law as interpreted by the rabbe, and also consulted him for advice on how to live in the modern world. My mother spoke disparagingly and perhaps with exaggeration about Pruve and her "eleven" children—"like a stairway, every two years," marking descending levels with her hand, down to the height of a small child: "boop boop boop, until the rebbe told her it was okay to get a ring," a euphemism for birth control. When I finally found a reference to the Adler family in the Czech census of 1930, it stated that the mother of the family, Pruve, had only been pregnant ten times. Perhaps the dispensation for birth control came in 1931.

* * *

My mother was also angry with the entire Weiss clan for stealing my father away from us twice a year. He loved spending Rosh Hashanah and Yom Kippur with his cousins, insisting that going to Williamsburg to be with them was like going home to Munkach. On top of that grudge, my mother felt that their worldview of what a "good" Jew was insulted her and her entire family, who were pious as well, but without following a charismatic single rebbe. The only evidence I heard from her to support this assertion was one incident: she and my father had entered a grocery store in Williamsburg, and a little boy behind the counter went running to the back of the store, shouting in Yiddish "the *goyim* are here," meaning he had mistaken my mother and father for non-Jews. At her insistence, my father eventually stopped visiting that side of the family, and the last I had seen of any of them was in 1975, when some of them had spoken at my father's funeral—in Yiddish.

I would have to re-create that family tree myself, and I had not lacked for family growing up. Since my mother was one of five siblings who lived in the New York area, and my father also had four siblings nearby, my childhood Sundays had been spent visiting family. The other six days of the week, no matter how lonely I felt or how often I was bullied at school,

I knew I was part of not one but *two* big, loving families, where I had my place in a busload of people who would know if I went missing. I had ten first cousins on my mother's side, ten on my father's. My mother was one of five Kaufman children—six if you count the brother who died when he slipped on ice and hit his head. The first three were born in a village in Podolia Gubernia, Ukraine, and moved to America in 1920. The younger three, including my mother, were born in the Bronx. They worked together in the fur-matching business—they had a shop in the garment district repairing the warmest of coats available in the days before more affordable polar fleece and Gore-Tex. They repaired coats from all over the country. My mother and her siblings spoke Litvak Yiddish to each other and ranged in Jewish practice from strictly Orthodox to left-wing atheist.

My father was one of eight Adler children (or nine, or ten, depending on what documents you followed) who had grown up in Munkach. One died as a baby. One went to Palestine sometime in the late 1930s or early '40s. Two died in the war, along with my grandparents and my father's first family. Bernard Weiss, the youngest brother of my grandmother Pruve, had fled the Hasidic life to come to America and marry his sweetheart in the 1920s. After the war he had brought over not only his sister Pruve's children, "the Adler Boys"—my father and his brothers Mendy, Willy, and Imi, and their sister Blanka, Sam Kahan's mother—but he had also brought over his sister Tziporah's children, Suri and Miriam. That whole branch of the family spoke Hungarian to each other, or Galician Yiddish with Hungarian accents.

It took me a long time to get that straight.

The next generation up the family tree from my father and his brothers centers around Pruve Weiss and her husband, Chaim David Adler. Chaim David had been to *yeshiva*, but joined the Austro-Hungarian Army in World War I and thereafter lived in the modern world without any help from the rebbe. Chaim David became a merchant and a taxi driver, and his five boys helped him in the business. My father, the eldest son, had to figure out how to keep his dad from wrecking cars, since Chaim David never quite understood that a car was not a horse and could not be turned, stopped, and jumped like one. My father tinkered with the gas pedal and engine to prevent my grandfather from wrecking the family's proudest possession—a Tatra Zenith automobile, modified to accommodate extra passengers. I still have the registration for that car.

Pruve Adler (née Weiss) of the Spinka Chasidic Weisses, was an observant Jewess. None of Pruve's children inherited her piety, although they got her dimples; I can see them in the mirror sometimes if I smile a certain way. However, the children of Pruve's sister Tziporah—Miriam Weiss (née Weider) and her sister Suri Lowy (née Weider)—were devoted to the Spinka rebbe and settled in Williamsburg, Brooklyn, where they lived as pious a life as they had lived in Europe.

As I continued my research, I reasoned that I should reconnect with the Spinka branch. They would have information I needed. After all, they had lived in Munkach with my father before the war and been deported to Auschwitz along with him. They might remember or have heard about his exploits after liberation. They might know the name of the family my father hid in the German garage, the family we had once visited in Brooklyn and who had given me a slice of birthday cake. Also, I smugly assumed they didn't have much of a life, living as they did in their Hasidic bubble. The past would be very important to them.

Again, my cousin Sam came to the rescue. He knew them well and had stayed in touch with them over the years. "Oh, such sweet people! Give them a call," he said, but as often as he gave me their number, I lost it and secretly hoped to understand their role in the family without actually having to meet them. Bernard's daughter-in-law told me that after sponsoring them and helping them get settled in the United States, her father-in-law had left them alone. "He had no use for those cousins. He called them all a bunch of *schnorrers*," "people who live off the charity of others," the daughter-in-law said. She sent me a clipping from a Jewish newspaper that detailed a federal investigation of the latest Spinka rebbe for tax fraud.

I researched their names, and in 2009 I found a listing for Miriam Weiss and called. The woman who answered the phone agreed that her name was Miriam Weiss and that her aunt had been named Pruve, but she didn't seem to welcome any further inquiry. Who was I and why was I bothering her, and could I repeat what I said?

She handed the phone to her daughter, Tziporah. "Oh, yes," said the daughter. "We knew the Adlers. They sent us nuts and chocolate before Pesach every year, and we would sell it and use the money to buy wine instead."

I ignored the *schnorrer* story and asked what else she remembered about my father. "I remember his wedding in the Bronx," she said. "And back in Munkach my mother used to play with his children."

She meant the children in the picture, Suri's children. She had known of my father through two of the lives he had lived.

"What was it like back then?" I asked.

"It was . . . a world in itself. We all lived together: religious, not religious, Jewish, not Jewish."

"What about when the Germans came?"

"Ach, it was terrible. Who wants to remember such things?"

This was not very helpful.

Two years after this conversation, I visited Miriam and her daughter, Tziporah, at her home in Brooklyn.

I gave the cabbie Miriam's address on Lee Avenue in Williamsburg. It was a neighborhood that could have used some paint. Although in more recent years Williamsburg has become a hip place for artists, it was traditionally the biggest enclave of Hasidim in New York City. The women in the street wear dark clothing and wigs, and many of them push multibaby carriages. The supermarkets have Yiddish and Hebrew signs in the windows. Even the empty bags blowing in the street have Hebrew lettering.

"Boy, there are a lot of Jews here," I said, sounding a little like my husband, with his "too many Israelis in Israel for me to visit there" comment.

I got out at a small brownstone building. Inside the unlocked vestibule it smelled stale and had buzzers for eight apartments. The stair treads were concave with wear. The only shiny thing in the hallway was the track for a recently installed wheelchair lift.

I heard a creak above me. An older woman with a brown wig and a hat appeared at the top of the stairs. "Miriam?" I asked, still adjusting to the dim light.

"Yes, up here."

I dragged my suitcase up the stairs and greeted Miriam and her daughter, Tziporah. The apartment was railroad style, long and narrow. A big dining table cluttered with old newspapers filled the one room that had good light. In the corner of the dining room was a glass case with silver objects—Kiddush cups and candelabras, mostly. A shelf held a mirror and small vases of artificial flowers. An old man sat stooped in a wheelchair parked at the head of the dining table before an open, large-print prayer book. He looked at me with the large round eyes of a Kewpie doll. He had *payyes*, *tzitit*, a *tallit*, and a *kippah*. He wore the two boxes held against the forehead and arm with leather straps called *t'fillin*, or "phylacteries." The black leather strap and the black box on his forehead stood out against his pale skin and white beard.

He sat very still, his eyes very round. It creeped me out. Men were supposed to put on *t'fillin* for the morning prayers, and then take them off and put them away, but it was already one o'clock in the afternoon. The man stared at me with an intensity I could not place.

Miriam ignored him. "Sit down, sit down," she said.

"Um, is this your husband?" I asked. "Is he allowed to talk to me?" Some Hasidim practice institutionalized separation of the sexes.

"No, no, he doesn't talk anymore," said Miriam. "Water on the brain or something."

Now I knew where I had seen someone staring like that—my friend Kate, after a catastrophic stroke.

I sat at the table and opened my laptop to show Miriam my pictures of Munkach. She knew some of the streets and houses. "Yes, I remember the Adlers well," she said. "They always sent us packages of nuts and chocolate before Pesach, and we would sell them to buy wine."

That story again. I was hoping for something fresh.

"What do you remember about my father and his first wife?" I asked.

"It was so long ago. Who remembers?" said Miriam. "Your grandfather, he had a heart of gold. He made the match between my husband and me. No one else thought first cousins should marry, but he said go ahead."

The front door opened without a knock, and another woman came in. Miriam hugged and kissed her and introduced her as her sister, Suri, a name I was never happy to hear.

This Suri acted like an older sibling. Her head was covered with a kerchief, and she carried herself with great dignity. She also carried a plastic shopping bag. "Here," she said, taking from it an inexpensive LCD alarm clock. "You are writing things down; you need to keep track of the time."

I thanked her, though puzzled by the gift.

"And here," she said, bringing out a magnetic notepad designed for a refrigerator and marked with the days of the week. "So you can keep track of what you need to do each day. If the pen runs out, here is another one." Suri reached back into the bag and produced one of those cheap four-color pens you give to children.

"Wow," I said, not sure whether this was all they could afford or all they thought of me, but I admired the way Suri had ennobled her humble collection of gifts with a narrative for how they might be used. My father's sister Batya had done that, too. Perhaps I could connect with these women by talking about Batya, who had passed away five years ago in a nursing home in Williamsburg, and who had lived upstairs from us in the Bronx with her accordion, and whose son was the Sam Kahan who had traveled with me to Ukraine. I thought this would be a good bridge to conversation, but Suri immediately launched into a story of her own. She drew herself up, took a deep breath, and looked off into the distance. "Why did we always eat challah with jam on Shabbos?" she asked me.

Because the rest of the week you had brown bread with nothing else, I thought, but it would have been rude to say so. "I don't know," I said. "Why?"

"My mother and father always kept their door open on Shabbos. When the Jewish soldiers got out of their . . . I don't know the word. . . ."

"Garrison? Base?"

"When they got out for dinner, they would look for a kosher meal and see our house. My mother would dump the *samovar* into the soup pot. You know what a *samovar* is?"

"A kettle."

"She would dump the water from the *samovar* into the soup, and the soldiers would get the meat and the *kugel*. My sister and I would have challah with jam instead, *so holy* were my parents."

"Well, they sound like good, generous people," I said, nodding, not sure what was expected of me.

"We had just finished our Seder when the Germans came and took us. I was seventeen, and my sister was fourteen."

I looked down at the table in silence. These were all the stories I was going to get from them, and it would have to be enough.

CHAPTER 18

Wrestling with Religion

My father's faith was as complicated as the political history of his town. Not very much has been written about Mukacheve or Munkach, this town in Carpathian Ruthenia on the banks of the Latoricza River. Much of my research is taken from my own experience, short entries in generalized encyclopedias of the region, sidebars in histories of Hungarian and Czech Jews, and personal memoirs, including the work of Simon Deutsch, who wrote and published an extensive memoir in Yiddish, which I had translated into English. Munkach was the main market town, surrounded by farmland and forestland so remote that their air and water remained pure, while the borders were muddy. Hungarian speakers, Ukrainian speakers, Russian speakers, Ruthenian speakers, German speakers, and Yiddish speakers all lived together. The town was close to the geographic center of the ancient Austro-Hungarian Empire, which ruled Munkach in 1911, when my father was born, from the twin capitals of Vienna and Budapest.

In the political upheaval that came during and after World War I and in accordance with the Treaty of Trianon in 1920, Munkach became part of a new country, Czechoslovakia, a politically utopian country that was ruled from Prague.

The Czechs were good governors but not sufficiently important to Germany, France, Italy, and England to prevent Neville Chamberlain from carving up the country and trying to pacify the Nazis with parts of its terri-

tory in the Munich Agreement of 1938. This gift included my father's town at the country's southern end. The Nazis wanted coal and steel, not farms, so after a ceremonial parade through their new lands, they formed an alliance with the rulers of Hungary and left rule of Carpathian Ruthenia, including Munkach, to them. It was the 1938 parade of the Germans that prompted my grandfather and many other men to put on their old World War I uniforms and have pictures taken so they could ingratiate themselves with their new rulers.

Cropped from original, found at the Holocaust Encyclopedia Online, hosted by the United States Holocaust Memorial Museum (www.ushmm.org). This map shows territories under Hungarian rule during World War II.

Munkach was mostly left alone from 1938 to 1944. Other towns were not so lucky.

United States Holocaust Memorial Museum

Towns under German rule were much tougher on their Jews. Jewish people began pouring into Munkach, fleeing from German *Aktions* in towns that used to be Poland, less than a hundred miles away. *Aktions* were effectively pogroms with automatic weapons, part of the attempt to make the countryside *Judenrien*, Jew free. This influx prompted the Hungarian administrators to deport all Jews who were seeking shelter in Munkach back to Poland and Germany and wherever they came from.

This is why my father carefully kept a statement from the city hall that he was a native of the town. That piece of paper kept him from being deported to the killing countries. In his testimony to the United Nations Relief and Rehabilitation Administration Restitution, my father claimed he was doing forced labor in Kaschau—the Hungarian word for Kosice, a town north of Munkach. But people with money could definitely buy their way out of the Munka Tabor, the Hungarian forced labor corps that existed during that time. And he testified that he was released on March 22, 1944, for one month, until he was captured in the Munkach ghetto, so I consider his whereabouts in that time to be fairly flexible, especially since forced labor brigades, under the Horthy regime, allowed leaves from time to time.

At least in the early years of Hungarian occupation of Munkach, my grandfather had some sort of understanding with the Hungarian bureaucrats. Between 1939 and 1942, at least, he was allowed to run his business, because my father's papers include a car registration that shows that Chaim David Adler was allowed to own a taxi.

Then, in the spring of 1944 after years of simple oppression and assaults on their livelihood, which the Jews under the rule of Hungary ignored or adjusted to, events moved like the lightning symbol on the SS uniforms. First, Hitler ghettoized the Jews of Hungary; then, he deported them, and in less than two months, the Jewish Community of Hungary was gone. If you've read Elie Wiesel's book *Night*, you know what happened in Munkach. Complacency, studied ignorance of the Germans' plan, followed by swift betrayal and death was the fate of Hungarian Jews during World War II.

The United States Holocaust Memorial Museum section on the German occupation of Hungary states the following:

> In April 1944, Hungarian authorities ordered Hungarian Jews living outside Budapest (roughly 500,000) to concentrate in certain cities, usually regional government seats. Hungarian gendarmes were sent into the rural regions to round up the Jews and dispatch them to the cities. The urban areas in which the Jews were forced to concentrate were enclosed and referred to as ghettos. Sometimes the ghettos encompassed the area of a former Jewish neighborhood. In other cases the ghetto was merely a single building, such as a factory.
>
> In some Hungarian cities, Jews were compelled to live outdoors, without shelter or sanitary facilities. Food and water supplies were dangerously inadequate; medical care was virtually non-existent. Hungarian authorities forbade the Jews from leaving the ghettos and police guarded the perimeters of the enclosures. Individual gendarmes often tortured Jews and extorted personal valuables from

them. None of these ghettos existed for more than a few weeks and many were liquidated within days.

DEPORTATION OF HUNGARIAN JEWS

In mid-May 1944, the Hungarian authorities, in coordination with the German Security Police, began to systematically deport the Hungarian Jews. SS Colonel Adolf Eichmann was chief of the team of "deportation experts" that worked with the Hungarian authorities. The Hungarian police carried out the roundups and forced the Jews onto the deportation trains.

In less than two months, nearly 440,000 Jews were deported from Hungary in more than 145 trains. Most were deported to Auschwitz, but thousands were also sent to the border with Austria to be deployed at digging fortification trenches. By the end of July 1944, the only Jewish community left in Hungary was that of Budapest, the capital.

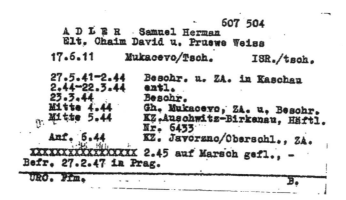

A summary of my father's wartime experiences as told to a representative of URO

Perhaps this is why the United Restitution Organization (URO) document above shows that my father was released from forced labor between February and March of 1944—he saw what was coming, talked his way out, took his family, and fled to the woods. But they made a fatal mistake. They visited the ghetto, which according to the Deutsch memoir was not yet tightly locked down, to celebrate Passover with parents and in-laws. They were subsequently detained there, then deported to Auschwitz, where my father was separated from his wife, two children, and his parents, never to see any of them again. He kept their memories alive by observing all of their *yahrzeits* on Hoshana Rabah, the seventh day of Sukkot, the harvest holiday that follows Yom Kippur, where you beat a set of willow branches until their leaves fall off. The bare branches left after the ritual must have reflected how alone he felt knowing his parents, wife, and children were dead. My father further memorialized his loss by keeping a portrait of his beloved murdered little girl where he could never forget her and thus burned that whole complex of memories into my subconscious, where I provided many therapists with income for decades.

How was my father's faith complicated? He observed as many commandments as he could, but broke the second commandment routinely. He put on his *t'fillin* and prayed every morning of his life, and then went to work on the Sabbath. My mother was always ashamed that my father worked on Saturday, while her father and brothers never did. But things were different for them. My mother's family worked in the "rag trade," a mostly Jewish enterprise where Jews set the rules. But my father was in the automotive business, and Saturday was when the men came to his place to buy car parts. Retail has always been strongest on Saturday, and he mostly worked alone in dealing with the public, so my father really had no choice. He took off work—meaning he closed his place—for Rosh Hashanah, Yom Kippur, and the first and last days of Pesach; he went to synagogue on the first and last days of Sukkot, and not much else. During his retirement, however, he proudly kept the *minyan* alive in our Conservative congregation, Midchester Jewish Center, by going every morning and getting his brothers and friends to show up, too. And after my father got sick, when he could no longer work or go to synagogue, reading the Psalms of David gave him great comfort. The Midchester Jewish community children were my friends; they were an important part of the crowd that surrounded me during my father's *shiva*.

So it was natural that my husband and I joined a Conservative congregation, even though we almost never went. We belonged to the Conservative congregation in Palo Alto for sixteen years, until after my first son's bar mitzvah, which I did not enjoy as much as I should have. The rabbi ignored all my requests and invited a controversial guest speaker I did not even know was going to speak. So I decided it was time to switch congregations. My younger son had friends in an unaffiliated congregation that happened to meet very close to my house, so I gave it a try. That is how I discovered the joys of *really* liberal Judaism at Congregation Etz Chayim.

My introduction to Etz was winning their Hamentashen cookoff in 2001, which encouraged me to have my second son's bar mitzvah there. I got drawn into the unconventional, unceremonious, irreverent aspects of Etz Chayim life while my son trained to read the Torah and recite his Haftorah. One such cheeky practice was the "Broadway Shabbat," a special alternative service, one of many such services, constructed for the unusual occurrence of a month with five Fridays.

"I have to write about this, if God doesn't strike us all dead before we finish," I remarked to my friend Jess, as we read the program for the service that night. The program was laid out to look like a theater program. The banner on the cover said "Praybill" instead of "Playbill."

"Oh, just relax and sing. It's great," Jess said.

The order of the service was listed on the cover, and they followed the usual progression of prayers, sort of. For the Broadway Shabbat, show tunes substituted for the traditional prayers. On the *bimah*, along with the reading table and ark and rabbi, were a percussionist, a pianist, and a choir dressed in black tie. One member of the choir with a deep, resounding voice explained that tonight we would be singing the words of Rabbis Gershwin, Hamlisch, and Herman and that Cole Porter was going to be given honorary membership in the tribe for the evening.

The congregation, dressed mostly in jeans, followed their lead and sang the following words to the tune of "Lullaby of Broadway":

> Come on along and listen to, the service on Fifth Friday
> The Amidah and Baruch'Hu, we're gonna do it "my way."

A few congregants were shocked into silence, and some were laughing too hard to sing, but most followed along, reading the annotations that explained what *feelings* the traditional prayers had and the logic behind how the show tunes were chosen to embody them.

We began singing Psalm 96 to the tune of "The Sound of Music":

> Sing to Adonay, sing a new song!
> Sing to *Adonay*, all the earth!

I thought about how odd it was that he had appropriated a song that had been associated with a convent. The melody of "Ol' Man River" came next, standing in for "Eli, Eli," a dirge written in the depths of the dark days of World War II, when the writer of the prayer expressed a simple hope for continuity of man and the natural world in the midst of that chaos. That is when things started to make more sense to me. To my surprise, welcoming the Sabbath Bride with "Hello Dolly" scanned well, and the song with reworked lyrics perfectly described the communal experience of worship,

> And now the room's swaying
> 'Cause we're all praying.

And the next song said, in a nutshell, "It is good to praise and thank Adonay," by having us all sing "There's No Business like Show Business" twice, first with the familiar tune and lyrics, then with the rewritten ones, where the Hebrew word *Sh-mo*—meaning "His (God's) name"—was substituted for "show," with some other substitutions.

When the next prayer, the one that praises the Almighty, who blends dawn into dusk, was replaced by "Night and Day" by Cole Porter, I was singing along with gusto. A few songs were kept in the original Hebrew, like the Sh'ma ("Hear Oh Israel, the Lord is our God, the Lord is one"), but we followed that up with "One" from *A Chorus Line*, even though "One" is sung about a female, and the Sh'ma is recited to a God who is usually considered male. At Congregation Etz Chayim, we have a lot of thinkers, including the rabbi, who believe that the Shekinah, the female aspect of the Divine, is as important as the male aspect. Perhaps that is because the rabbi has four daughters.

I feel that some core tenets of Judaism—which include doubt, bargaining, hospitality, questioning, and love of the stranger—are necessary and universal, and Etz embodies those values without shutting out secular values or people from other religions. This congregation acknowledges that two Jews can be a mixed marriage. I needed that, because as I got more and more involved, my husband grew more and more scornful. The turn of the twenty-first century brought out the most militant tendencies of believers and nonbelievers.

I would have preferred not to act out those roles in my own home. Unfortunately, I had no choice. Over the kitchen table, in the bathroom getting ready for the day, or anywhere my husband had left a copy of *Scientific American*, *Free Inquiry*, the *Skeptical Inquirer* or a host of other publications on the subject, the two of us often debated the topic of religions. I would maintain the position that religions were necessary and benign, as long as they did not gravitate into fanaticism. My husband took the position that all religion was evil, even liberal religion.

CHAPTER 19

Up the River with the Atheists

Every so often, my husband hosts gatherings of people he meets in his skeptical, antireligion pursuits. They sit in my living room and discuss physics and religion and how God should be taken off US currency and the phrase "one nation under God," which was added because of the Cold War, should be taken out of the Pledge of Allegiance. On one of these evenings, I overheard my husband taking his friends on a tour through our library. "Here's my section of science books," he told them. "Over there, Preeva's Jewish books." Then he said something else, but I could only make out the words "she" and "amazing."

"Honey?" I asked him later that night. "What were you saying to your friends in the library?"

I would have loved to hear him say he was proud of me for pursuing my Jewish interests while leaving him free to pursue his atheism, or that my collection of Judaica was impressive, or something—anything—nice.

"I don't remember," is all he said.

It reminds me of all he forgets. He forgets that together we have shared many memorable experiences, particularly those where I helped him indulge his lifelong passion for all things space and astronomy. Our first weekend away together was on Nantucket, where we got up in the middle of the night and drove to the darkest part of the island to see the moon turn copper as a new penny. After we were married in 1984, we chased an annular solar eclipse through a park in Virginia. In 1991, we took a special vacation to the Big Island of Hawaii for a total eclipse. We made special arrangements so we could leave our cozy condo at 3 a.m. and ride a bus to sit on the grounds at the Waikoloa Stables on the island of Hawaii to see a lunar eclipse, surrounded by hundreds of eclipse-oholics with their sleeping bags, pup tents, coolers, and beach chairs. Some even brought their Celestron telescopes, which proved that they were wealthier than their grooming or attire would indicate. I was in charge of recording the proceedings on videotape. "It's totality now," you can hear me say in voice-over. "It's very dark. It's very cold. Still cloudy."

My husband, who trained as an experimental astrophysicist, showed everyone who came to the house his certificate and patch from STS-3, the third flight of the space shuttle, which contained in its cargo bay the experiment he designed for the Columbia Astrophysics Lab as part of his doctoral work. He and his fellow graduate students built something that looked like a garbage can with windows to measure the polarization of x-rays from the sun, and part of the shuttle's mission was to open the doors of the cargo bay and allow this and other experiments to run.

Len's one regret was that he was in Houston during that launch and never saw it in person. At an October 1998 auction for the San Jose Symphony, I saw a chance to make it right. I bid on a last-minute item donated by Lockheed Martin—a trip to Cape Canaveral to see a shuttle launch. "Over here!" I yelled, raising my paddle.

"Are you crazy? Don't bid on that," Len protested.

"I'm not bidding; I'm buying," I said serenely.

For our $5,000, we all went down to Florida for ringside seats in the viewing stands at the Kennedy Space Center, so we could see the shuttle take off.

After many astronomical-centered trips, I was ready to look at the Earth for a change. In spring 2008, I agreed to go with him on a trip to the Amazon River sponsored by the Center for Inquiry (CFI), the organization that published his favorite magazine, the *Skeptical Inquirer*. CFI was chartering an entire riverboat in Brazil to visit the rain forests. The Amazonian rain forests have been called the lungs of the Earth; presumably, the top management of this nonprofit, who were all traveling to Brazil from Buffalo, wanted to check on the patient. Lectures on secularism and science were advertised as part of the appeal of the trip. I had had quite enough lectures on secularism at home, but I was willing to sit through a few more of them for the pleasure of seeing the plant life in the Amazon. Nevertheless I was a bit worried about spending so much time in the company of skeptics. I did not want to get into debates with them, too. On the other hand, I told myself, as I authorized the large credit card charges involved, it would be good to get Leonard out on vacation. Retired as he was, my husband never felt like having a vacation. Except for family reunions and trips to view total solar eclipses and rocket launches, he stayed put.

As photos from the brochure suggested, we turned out to be the youngest couple on the trip. The others all thought we were adorable, even when we bickered over what kind of juice was in the dispenser at breakfast. The ship was like a miniature floating apartment building—a modern, urban one, with terraces. The most important feature was that the rooms were well air-conditioned, because the Amazon, no surprise, was *hot*. It was humid, too. We were floating on the shallow humidifier of the world. Once the ship left the port of Manaus, it never docked, just sat anchored in the middle of the river, while we took motorized launches for all our excursions. In our padded orange life jackets and other gear, we looked like tangerines with hats as we motored up and down the backwaters, under trees with orchids growing on the trunks and sloths hanging from branches and to special research stations where the pink Amazon dolphins ate from our hands.

The outings were fascinating, but the guests of honor were better. The primary speaker was the avuncular and charming Paul Kurtz, a philosopher who was the originator and chair of CFI. Kurtz brought along his youngest child, a college junior who brought a welcome energy to the group. She turned twenty-one on the trip. The evening of her twenty-first birthday, I was sitting with her and her father at a bar on the top deck. The bartender made her a "special birthday drink"—a *caipirinha* (a drink of mint, ice, sugar, and the Brazilian rum called *cachaca*) with an inch of extra-strong rum floating on the top, to which he set fire.

The challenge was to drink the burning rum before the straw melted. The birthday girl succeeded.

"You know, fire is very important in many Jewish rituals," I observed to Kurtz. "Do you know what Havdalah is?"

"The ritual on Saturday night, right?" he said. Kurtz was born Jewish. Every week for Havdalah, I told him, my father would make the blessing over a shot of brandy, pour it into a saucer, and light it. He would make a big show of dipping his fingers into the burning brandy and putting his hand in his pocket, as if putting fire there, for good luck. He also put some on my head for intelligence and good grades. "It had a powerful effect on me," I said. "You should figure out an atheist ritual with fire sometime."

"How about you try drinking this drink?" Kurtz said. So I did, without the straw melting.

Steven Pinker, an eminent psychology professor from MIT, was another star presenter. His wife, Rebecca Newberger Goldstein, a philosopher and author who had won a MacArthur Genius Grant, presented as well, and her talks were more interesting than her husband's. I got to hang out a bit with Pinker and Newberger Goldstein, and the whole ship benefited from their gracious presence. They were the epitome of intellectuals in love—crediting each other in their talks and spending hours together on a banquette outside their stateroom as they worked on separate laptops while leaning against each other. In all ways they presented the very picture of marital bliss and intellectual partnership.

They were also wicked smart. Pinker had just been on the *Colbert Report*, where the host asked him to sum up his book *How the Mind Works* in five words. "Brain cells fire in patterns," Pinker said, summing up a complex subject on the spot.

In Pinker's lectures aboard the CFI ship, he looked at individual words and patterns of how people spoke, just as a scientist would. He separated words from their usage at different times in history, as if putting them in jars of formaldehyde at various stages of development. By contrast, his wife's talks were like a cool swim in the refreshing waters of the language Pinker analyzed. In her readings from her then soon-to-be-published book, *36 Arguments for the Existence of God: A Work of Fiction*, Newberger Goldstein described a fictional professor of psychology named Cass Seltzer who experienced philosophical epiphanies similar to the ones I had experienced, resulting in a profound feeling of gratitude for personal good fortune.

In my case, gratitude came along with a massive side order of survivor guilt. I sometimes felt so grateful it hurt. Going to Saturday services was one of the few ways to ease that pain, keeping alive the heritage for which my half-siblings had died. Why did my husband have to make fun of me for doing it? Why couldn't he and I be a couple like Rebecca and Steven—two viewpoints, two laptops, but warmly supporting each other all the same?

I discussed it with them (for the duration of the trip, they were Steven and Rebecca—such a thrill for me!) one afternoon over lunch. "Do you think I can be Jewish *and* be married to a born-again atheist?" I asked. "I'd like to think it's possible."

They looked at each other. "Personally, I don't see a problem," Steven said. "The two of us are atheists who were married under a huppah."

I felt vindicated. After that, I stopped having my *Fiddler on the Roof*–style nightmare where I was getting married in a *shtetl* and found myself separated from my groom by a wall of atheist manifestos, never to get close to him, ever.

On the trip up the Amazon with the atheists, Leonard was more vital than I had seen him in years. He jumped out of bed in the morning and was prowling the three decks looking for conversation with like-minded people before I was awake. On that ship, where we were isolated from the rest of the world, Len was his best self. Part of it was being among atheists, but I also think it was because of his love of the sky.

When you're on a ship in the middle of the Amazon, there is a lot of sky. Six of the seven nights we were on the river, there were clouds, which made for fabulous sunsets but bad stargazing, but one night we had wonderful conditions. The sky was cloudless and still. That night, with the Southern Cross setting close to one horizon and the Big Dipper rising close to the other, my husband went to the top deck with a star atlas and a green laser pointer. He began pointing out astronomical objects to a man born and raised in São Paulo—so far south of the equator he had never seen the Big Dipper—and the two of them talked the crew into launching a motor-boat for a more unobstructed view. All the people Len had been chatting up on the cruise, including Steven and Rebecca, piled into the boat. We coasted into a still inlet and shut off our lights so our eyes could adapt to the dark. As the ripples from the boat's passage died down, we saw an extraordinary sight. The Milky Way reflected perfectly onto the black water and came right up to the side of the boat; then it took off into the sky.

Einstein supposedly said, "There are only two ways to live your life. One is as though nothing is a miracle. The other is as though everything is a miracle." We all said our private hallelujahs at the wonder of that sight and the immensity of the galaxy. I, for one, thanked God for the miracle of putting me in that place, in that moment.

CHAPTER 20

The Mystics of Elkins Park

My friend Valerie lives for two things: maintaining her exalted frequent-flyer status on United and getting other people to travel with her while she does that.

"Hey, Preeva, United has a sale to Australia," she'll say.

"Not interested."

A week later, she would be at it again: "There's a special fare to Hong Kong. We can leave Monday and be back in time for Shabbat!"

"Leave me alone."

I had traveled on my own a lot by 2011, but I still considered air travel a nightmare. I hated leaving my cozy little town of Palo Alto for anything but the most important trip, but in July 2011, Valerie finally persuaded me to rent a house with her for a Jersey Shore vacation. My initial skepticism had turned to pleasure when I saw that almost every house had at least one porch and that Cape May was built in a more genteel era than the New Jersey I had lately seen depicted on reality television shows. Dolphins played in the ocean just out of reach, and no gratuitous fried food was to be seen—only soft custard ice cream. Hansom cabs clopped along the streets. Gas lamps illuminated the Victorian houses in the evening with a soft glow. It was like San Francisco but without the hills and the parking problems.

Valerie also invited another friend to the shore house—Rayzel Raphael, the first person I'd ever met from Elkins Park, Pennsylvania. I first became curious about Elkins Park when I bought a meditation rug and pillows on eBay from a man there who had commissioned weavers in the mountains of Iraq to create Persian carpets with Jewish themes. He was selling off the last of his inventory, which he had commissioned "to sell to all the wealthy women of Elkins Park who are into Zen and personal empowerment," he explained to me in an e-mail.

"I thought it's Californians who are into cosmic things like running with the wolves," I wrote back.

"The women here not only run with the wolves, commune with spirits, and read their chakras," he responded, "they also do yoga."

The guy with the rugs was right. Rayzel was a yoga-doing, wolf-running, chakra-mapping gal with a Southern accent, oversized gold jewelry, and a cloud of dark hair. She was a freelance Reconstructionist rabbi who sold Juice Plus vitamins out of her home, and ended every e-mail with prayers to the three gossamer spirits she believed watched over the Internet. She primarily performed weddings; but had two side projects: creating "Shekinah cards," a set of tarot-like cards that helped you get in touch with the female manifestation of the Divine, and composing a performance piece for the Philadelphia Fringe Festival called "Kabbalah, the Musical."

"You should really meet Elise, my *akashic* healer," she told me over her dairy-and-gluten-free lunch. *Akashic* means "records of past lives that don't exist on a physical plane." Elise claimed to have the ability to read them and fix whatever ailed you, and Rayzel swore by her. "I had a rotator cuff problem and I tried everything—physical therapy, massage, cortisone shots," she said. "Then Elise read my past and discovered I had been carrying some heavy burdens from back then. She helped me clear them up, and my shoulder got better right away."

"You're joking," I said, but I was intrigued.

"No, really, look at my arm now; it's fine," Rayzel said, reaching over her head with no apparent effort. "Elise can really help you figure out what it is you need and want."

I could hear the wolves howling in the distance, yet I felt that Rayzel had hit on a terrible problem I had with living my life. I had seen a total of eight therapists to try to fix this problem and was never done with them, only dismissed. Each time, we ended with the therapist either retiring from practice or saying, "I can't do anything more for you until you decide what you want."

I could never decide what I wanted. I couldn't even decide how to end my week on Cape May. Leave early and avoid traffic? Stay and have more time on the beach? Should I go and see Elkins Park itself, or not? Valerie overbooked herself all the time, obsessively checking her calendar to see what other activities she could fit in, and it didn't bother her at all. It was how she had managed to get a rabbinical degree and a chaplain's certificate after her children left home, plus a part-time job at the Veterans Affairs hospital in Palo Alto. Overbooking is Valerie's way of staying organized and she manages brilliantly.

But I'm not Valerie, who walked around neatening up our vacation condo, putting items I had not noticed were out of place back in order. It was like rooming with Mary Poppins—things flew back into place as if by magic.

When Rayzel invited me to visit her and Elise, I wanted to go. I wanted to see what magic they had in Elkins Park, so I said yes, but there was a problem—I already had reservations at my first genealogy conference in Washington, DC, where I was to see Rabbi Shmuley. I fought the familiar feeling of self-loathing that rose at the back of my throat every time I discovered I had double-booked myself. The voices in my head railed at me: "See! You never amounted to anything because you don't know what you're doing! Idiot!" After much agitation and self-flagellation, I decided we should leave Cape May early and make a stopover at Rayzel's house in Elkins Park, and then catch the express train to DC. I wanted to see the she-wolf lair for myself and maybe get a past-life reading. Rayzel lived in a stately stone house that looked as if it had been built by a Hanoverian duke. Inside were fine wood floors and walls covered with masks and shelves holding menorahs, Sephardic good luck charms, Stars of David, and depictions of angels. The kitchen's laminated counters were piled with Juice Plus supplies.

In the study, Rayzel gestured toward a line of cards spread out face down on a low table. "Pick one; see what it says," she commanded.

Obediently, I turned over a card. It said, "Trust the Divine Plan. Are you letting past hurts and failures occupy too much mental and emotional space?"

It was as if someone had looked into my heart and seen my greatest pain: I make mistakes. I always make mistakes.

I turned over another card—and then another.

> *Your soul's lesson: Review your life with appreciation and respect. As difficult as it may be to trust every episode and challenge you have faced, they have been essential facets of your journey, and none has been a mistake. Love who you are today and all that has contributed to your evolution.*
>
> *You are right on schedule.*

How could I be right on schedule? It seemed as if my entire life had been spent running away from a schedule. When I married at twenty-five, I left my little job and big, interesting family to move out west where no one knew me. I had buried my college ambition to become a writer under layers of motherhood, never had the guts to insist to my husband on having more than two children, and put on an extra eighty pounds of frustration weight. I waited so long to forge closer ties with my own big family that everyone had died or scattered. In my travels to my father's homeland, I was stung, not only by nettles, but by the feeling that certain details of his life only added up if there was a dishonest element to it, like smuggling or collaboration—how else had he stayed so prosperous in a desperate time? Now this tarot card was telling me that everything had transpired in the right order, as if I had orchestrated my life with prescient wisdom. I felt like I had spent the last thirty years of my life frozen in a frame of resentment about my father's sad fate, never progressing beyond a teenager in mental age.

The cacophony of voices in my head got louder. Tears rolled down my cheeks. I thought of the girl on the wall, the years spent in therapy, the endless research, the fruitless trips to Israel and Ukraine. I thought of the cousins who could not seem to hear my questions and how my own stubbornly selective memory often erased what was most important.

Rayzel put her arms around me and patted me on the back. "Oh, it's been a hard one, hasn't it?" she said.

EPILOGUE

Adler Hershi's Tochter

Right after Sam Kahan and I visited Ukraine, to preserve and share what I had seen and learned in my travels to Munkach, Budapest, and Prague, I put together a spiral-bound picture book. It contained snapshots of the streets and houses where the Adlers had lived, along with family photos from the American and Israeli branches of the Adler family in different countries over the years, up to the present day. While I was working on the picture book, I received an invitation to a cousin's wedding in Israel, so I brought copies for them and read it to the bridal party the night before the wedding, translating it into my bad Hebrew as I read. I also took a copy to Tziporah and Miriam in Williamsburg, Brooklyn, and the book opened doors for me, even in that Hasidic enclave.

Shortly after that, I had to make a life decision. My synagogue had asked me to volunteer as executive vice president, and in a year, move up to president. It was a big job, and I wasn't sure I could or wanted to do it, even though I went to synagogue and prayed often. I had found that, although I was still Jewish through and through, I no longer put my faith in a "big daddy" in the sky. The laws of the universe were awesome enough for me to treat them as a stand-in for a deity.

I wrote to Rebecca Newberger Goldstein from the Amazon trip about it. She assured me that plenty of Jews had been atheists for hundreds of years and that this ideological concern should not stop me from playing a major role in my congregation. I was still concerned, though, about how my personality traits would play out in such an environment, since I tend toward impatience and can be sarcastic and biting. Would I go crazy from the endless meetings and phone calls and e-mails, most of them on trivial matters? Was I up to the challenge of playing a role in other people's profound life-cycle events—births, deaths, and marriages? How would I handle it?

I thought about a story my cousin Sam Kahan told about my father. In the early days of the state of Israel, when kibbutzim formed the border between the new state and the surrounding Arab states, my dad had the job of going around to check on their defenses. At one place, he felt fairly certain that the machine guns in the guard towers had come from a shipment wherein the British had removed the firing pins. If so, those guns were useless, and the settlement was undefended.

The kibbutzniks, full of the arrogance of ignorance, assured my father that their defenses were strong, since they had read a book on the subject. My father invited them to try to shoot him, and after much back and forth, the kibbutzniks in the guard towers did pull their triggers.

The guns failed to fire.

Sam asked my father one question: "Uncle, what if they had fixed their guns and you didn't know it?"

"Then I'd be dead," my father told him, shrugging his shoulders.

Who will tell the stories of my father if not me? Where will my children, and my friends' children, learn about the history of the Jews, their history, if not from the storytellers who hand these tales down generation to generation, a job we have given to rabbis and religious school teachers today?

I saw then that my duty to my ancestors was clear. Yes, I might make mistakes. Yes, I might take a few shortcuts. Perhaps my father had made mistakes and taken shortcuts in the years between 1939 and 1944. Perhaps he had been a smuggler. But he lived his life with joy and integrity, was loved, and died with no regrets. He came from a family that worked with their hands and were not afraid to use their fists. He and his brothers were the tough guys of their town in Czechoslovakia. As youths, they stole fruit and broke windows and raced motorcycles. As they got older, they drove taxis and protected their fellow Jews. My father might have smuggled coffee and alcohol and rubber tires during the war, but he and his brothers also smuggled Jews out of German territory to safety behind battle lines, and my father had personally saved a family of fellow Jews by creating a shelter in a German garage and finding a caretaker for these Jews after he moved on to hide in the woods himself.

I was proud to be Hershi Adler's *tochter*. The father I knew had been true to himself, to the best of his ability, and he lived with and worked around his faults. So would I. As president of my synagogue in 2012, I held the Torah during Kol Nidre. Fighting back tears, I asked for communal forgiveness and a good year. I didn't have any magical powers, but I did have a clear vision and wish for my family and community to grow and prosper. It would have to be enough.

Glossary of Foreign Terms

Yiddish

bubbeh, bubi. Grandmother.

bubbeleh. Term of endearment, "little one."

Du redst nish kine richtigier Yiddish. You don't speak proper Yiddish.

fleishig. Deriving from meat, as in the German word *Fleish*. Food that contains mixed dairy products and meat is not kosher.

gatkes. Underwear.

Gay gezint, und kim gezint, adonay matzliach darkehcha. Go out well, come back well, and may God send you luck on your path.

goniffs. Thieves.

Igen, migen, hopp de fliegn. A nonsense phrase: "Yes, I don't know" in Hungarian, plus "catch the flies" in Yiddish.

kapo. A Jewish prisoner who worked for the Nazis in the concentration camp; traitor.

killeh. Hernia.

kleine, de. The little one.

mashinke. Little machine.

payyes. Sidelocks.

rebbe. Rabbi held in mystical esteem.

rosh. The head of the camp.

schmek. To smell.

schnorrers. People who live off the charity of others.

sheer. Actual transliteration is *Shee-oor*; a teaching on a Jewish subject.

sheester. Literally a shoemaker; someone who is not a deft practitioner of his trade.

shiksas. Non-Jewish women.

shul. House of prayer.

tchotchkes. Knickknacks.

tochter. Daughter.

umshlagplatz. Deportation plaza.

Yahrtzeit. Literally "year-time"; the anniversary of a death, when a twenty-four hour votive candle is lit.

Y'mach shmo. His name should be blotted out.

zaide. Grandfather.

Hebrew

Beit Din. A rabbinic court.

bimah. Stage for rabbi and Torah.

chalutzim. Pioneers.

daven. To pray.

Etzel. A secret army that operated before Palestine became Israel.

goyim. Non-Jews.

haroset. A dish made of apples, walnuts, wine, and cinnamon; eaten at Passover Seder.

Hasidim. Jews who follow a rebbe.

Havdalah. Saturday night ritual for the end of the Sabbath.

Hoshana Rabah. Seventh day of Sukkot.

huppah. Bridal canopy, marriage canopy.

Kaddish. Song to honor the dead.

kibbutz. Communal settlement in Israel with shared work and profits.

kippah. Skullcap, plural *kippot*.

Kol Nidre. Prayer for forgivenesses that begins Yom Kippur.

madrichim. Counselors.

menorahs. Candleholders for Hanukkah, with nine candles.

mikveh. Ritual bath.

minyan. The quorum of ten Jewish male adults required for certain religious obligations.

Pru u'rvu ee melu et ha'aretz. Be fruitful and multiply and develop the earth.

Purim. Festive spring holiday.

shiva. A seven-day period of formal mourning observed after the funeral of a close relative.

Shoah. Tragedy; modern term for Holocaust.

sicha. Discussion group.

sukkah. The temporary outdoor structure for Sukkot, the fall harvest festival.

tallit. Prayer shawl.

Tashlich. A ritual of casting away your sins for the year and starting the new year pure.

t'fillin. Phylacteries; a set of small black leather boxes containing scrolls of parchment inscribed with verses from the Torah, which are worn by observant Jews during weekday morning prayers.

tzitzit. Fringes; found at the corners of a *tallit* and on a fringed garment worn beneath the shirt by observant Jews.

yeshivot. Hebrew schools; plural form of *yeshiva*.

Yisgadal v'yisgdash, shmey robbo. Magnified and consecrated be the great name (first line of the Kaddish prayer).

Yom Kippur. Holiest day of the Jewish year, occasion for fasting and praying.

zachor. To remember.

Hungarian

Nem to do madjaru beselnyi. I don't speak Hungarian.

Russian

Kak po zhe vay it cheh, tovarish?. How are you, Comrade?

Ocheen kharasho, nichivo. Pretty good, I don't know.

A zopahd pitchok meen da nedet. Slavic or Russian curse involving mother's vagina.

Sanskrit

akashic. Records of past lives that don't exist on a physical plane.

APPENDIX 1

Family Relationships

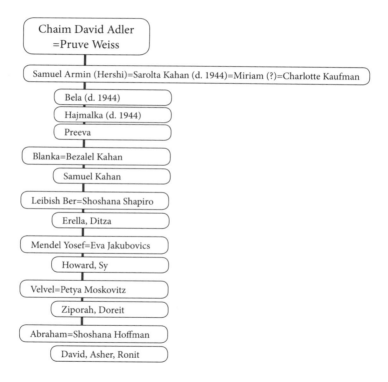

Chaim David Adler
=Pruve Weiss

Samuel Armin (Hershi)=Sarolta Kahan (d. 1944)=Miriam (?)=Charlotte Kaufman

Bela (d. 1944)

Hajmalka (d. 1944)

Preeva

Blanka=Bezalel Kahan

Samuel Kahan

Leibish Ber=Shoshana Shapiro

Erella, Ditza

Mendel Yosef=Eva Jakubovics

Howard, Sy

Velvel=Petya Moskovitz

Ziporah, Doreit

Abraham=Shoshana Hoffman

David, Asher, Ronit

Two generations of Adler descendants

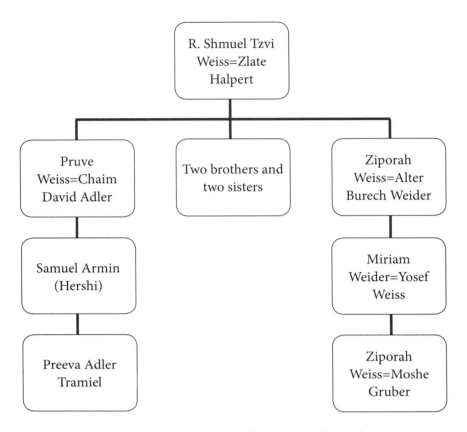

Family connection between Preeva Adler Tramiel and Ziporah Weiss

APPENDIX 2

Photographs

Charlotte, my mother, as a young woman

Shmuel Tzvi Adler, a.k.a. Adler Hershi, with his tow truck in Haifa in 1947

My father with an unnamed Israeli general, circa 1950–56

Ludwig, Imi, and Samuel Adler in 1947

My parents' wedding in 1957 in the Bronx

The Spinka Hasidim celebrating at my parents' wedding

My father selling motorcycles at an auto show in 1956

My father holding me on the roof of our building

Adler family, 1962

Samuel Adler with Crestwood Lake in the background, Yonkers, 1970s

Me with my father at the Wailing Wall, 1968

At Sy's bar mitzvah, 1970

Sam Kahan and Preeva Adler Tramiel, in the town we think was Vysni Apsa in 2010

Gypsies in Mukacheve across from the first apartment
Samuel Armin Adler shared with Suri

One entrance to the multifamily dwelling at 50 Korosveg, Mukacheve, 2010.
This is the second address I had for Samuel and Suri Adler.

Last recorded address for Samuel and Suri Adler, 58 Korosveg, Mukachevem, 2010

Entrance of 48 Havlickova Street, where the Adlers grew up, Mukacheve, 2010

Backyard of the house where the Adlers grew up, Mukacheve, 2010

Miriam Weider Weiss, Joseph Weiss, and Tziporah Weiss Gruber, 2013

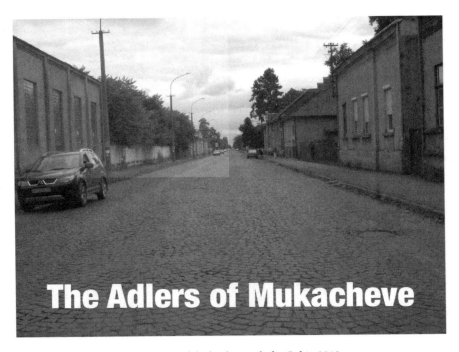

Front cover of the book I made for Gal in 2010

About the Author

Preeva Adler Tramiel is a writer, stand-up comic, gardener, community activist in California, and ex-officio president of the independent Congregation Etz Chayim. Her work has appeared in such publications as the *New York Observer*; *Judaism: A Quarterly Journal of Jewish Thought*; and the *Bay Daily News*, where she wrote the weekly "School Matters" column for three years. Online, she is a "Jewess with Attitude" on the Jewish Women's Archive blog, and on her websites, Preeva.net and Onecakebaker. com. An alumna of Barnard College, she appeared as a contestant on the television game show *Win Ben Stein's Money* (for which she won a consolation prize).

This book, under the name *Shadow Sister*, was a finalist in the 2014 Memoir Discovery Contest held by She Writes Press.